Weather Sense
Moisture

Author
Ann Wiebe

Illustrator
Margo Pocock

Editor
Betty Cordel

Desktop Publisher
Tanya Adams

Meteorological Consultant
Lawrence Greiss
National Weather Service
Hanford, California

Acknowledgments

Initial Idea Team
John Carmean
Betty Cordel
Dan Freeman
Tom Kelly
Linda Stansfield

Contributing Author
Betty Cordel

Contributions to "It's Snowing!"
Monica Hartman
Linda Stansfield

Additional Technical Illustrations
Michelle Pauls

This book contains materials developed by the AIMS Education Foundation. **AIMS** (**A**ctivities **I**ntegrating **M**athematics and **S**cience) began in 1981 with a grant from the National Science Foundation. The non-profit AIMS Education Foundation publishes hands-on instructional materials (books and the monthly magazine) that integrate curricular disciplines such as mathematics, science, language arts, and social studies. The Foundation sponsors a national program of professional development through which educators may gain both an understanding of the AIMS philosophy and expertise in teaching by integrated, hands-on methods.

ISBN 1-932093-00-1
Printed in the United States of America

Weather Sense
Moisture
Table of Contents

Introduction

As we wake in the morning, our thoughts turn to the day ahead. We peek out the window, read the paper, or turn on a newscast. Do I need a coat today? A scarf or mittens? An umbrella? Sunscreen? Will school start late because of fog or snow? Will the baseball game be cancelled due to rain? Weather affects people of all ages.

Children experience weather on a very personal level. It is tangible; it is relevant to their lives. This atmospheric laboratory is always present and available to tap their curiosity, whether testing the truth of historical proverbs (the earliest weather forecasters), measuring weather elements, or making sense of weather patterns.

Weather Sense: Moisture and its companion publication, *Weather Sense: Temperature, Air Pressure, and Wind,* are built around direct observation at a local site. Students will discover evidence of the unequal heating of Earth, the big idea behind weather, as they begin a lifetime journey toward comprehending why this is so. On the first level, attention is given to the particular key question in the activity being investigated. On the next level, the outcome of the investigation is related to the bigger essential question that drives a section of study. At an even higher level, it is hoped students will begin to relate the elements of weather—temperature, air pressure, wind, moisture—to each other. As they navigate through middle school and beyond, understanding the complexities of weather will involve connecting the physical sciences (heat energy, force and motion) and the earth sciences (solar system) and geography.

The ocean of air surrounding Earth is constantly on the move, but not always predictable. A barely perceptible change in one variable can ripple through the atmosphere, triggering a shift from the expected to the unexpected—from warm to cool, from breezy to gale force, from dry to wet. Weather can be harsh, but it can also be beautiful. It is cause for wonder.

> When we contemplate the whole globe as one great dewdrop, striped and dotted with continents and islands, flying through space with all the other stars, all singing and shining together as one, the whole universe appears as an infinite storm of beauty. This grand show is eternal. It is always sunrise somewhere; the dew is never all dried at once; a shower is forever falling; vapor ever rising. Eternal sunrise, eternal sunset, eternal dawn and gloaming, on seas and continents and islands, each in its turn, as the round earth rolls.
>
> John Muir (1838-1914) from *My First Summer in the Sierra*

The Big Picture

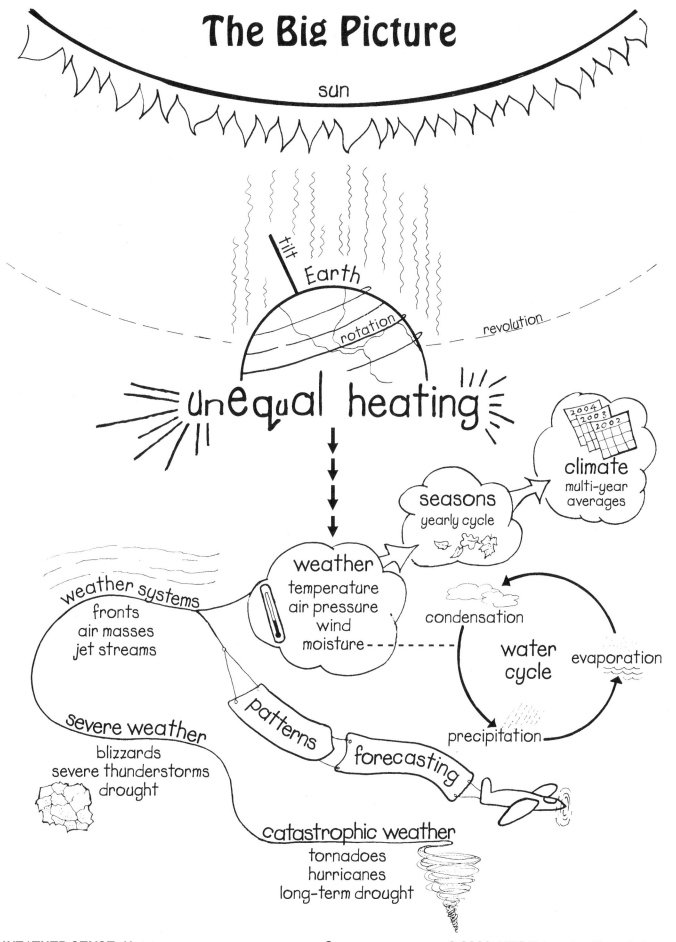

sun

tilt

Earth

rotation

revolution

unequal heating

climate
multi-year
averages

seasons
yearly cycle

weather
temperature
air pressure
wind
moisture

weather systems
fronts
air masses
jet streams

condensation

water
cycle

evaporation

precipitation

patterns

forecasting

severe weather
blizzards
severe thunderstorms
drought

catastrophic weather
tornadoes
hurricanes
long-term drought

Weather Close Up

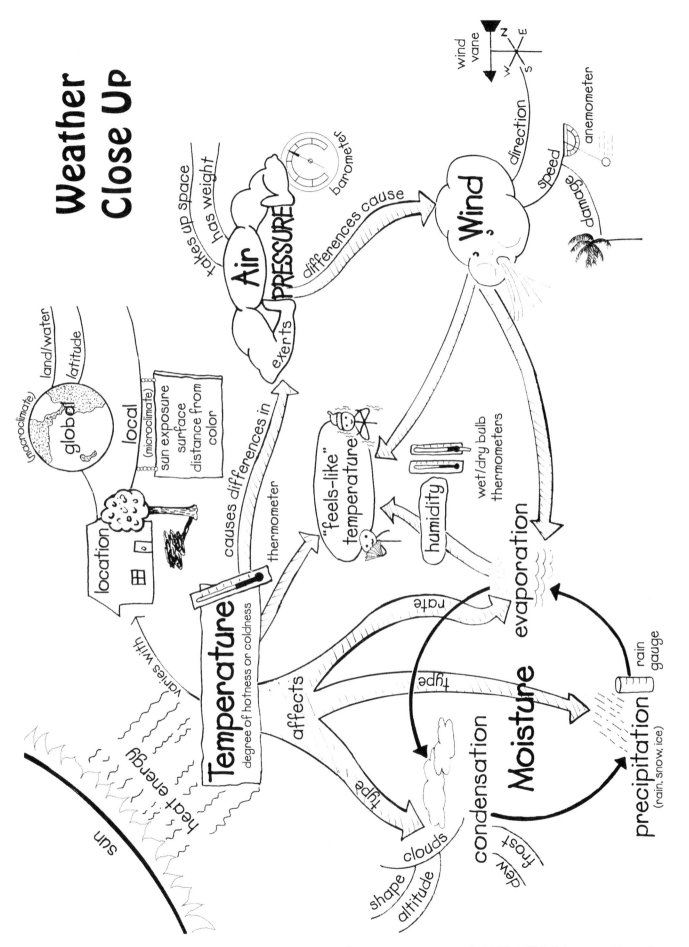

Weather Sense
Learning Goals

Investigate how the unequal heating of the Earth drives weather—temperature, air pressure, wind, and moisture.

- Observe and gather evidence that temperature varies with location, both locally and globally.

- Observe and gather evidence of the properties of air, the medium in which weather exists.

- Observe and gather evidence that wind varies in direction and speed.

- Observe and gather evidence that water endlessly cycles through evaporation (humidity), condensation (clouds and dew), and precipitation (rain and snow), causing a variety of weather conditions.

- Construct and/or use meteorological tools, such as thermometers, psychrometers, anemometers, and barometers, to quantify observations.

- Determine daily, weekly, and seasonal weather patterns for your location.

- Begin to understand how the four elements of weather—temperature, air pressure, wind, and moisture—interact with each other.

 More specific learning goals for the individual weather elements are found on the assessment pages.

National Education Reform Documents

The AIMS Education Foundation is committed to remaining at the cutting edge of providing curriculum materials that are user-friendly, educationally sound, developmentally appropriate, and aligned with the recommendations found in national education reform documents.

NRC Standards*

Science as Inquiry
- *Plan and conduct a simple investigation.*
- *Employ simple equipment and tools to gather data and extend the senses.*
- *Use appropriate tools and techniques to gather, analyze, and interpret data.*
- *Communicate investigations and explanations.*
- *Simple instruments, such as magnifiers, thermometers, and rulers, provide more information than scientists obtain using only their senses.*

Physical Science
- *Materials can exist in different states—solid, liquid, and gas. Some common materials, such as water, can be changed from one state to another by heating or cooling.*

Earth and Space Science
- *The sun, moon, stars, clouds, birds, and airplanes all have properties, locations, and movements that can be observed and described.*
- *Weather changes from day to day and over the seasons. Weather can be described by measurable quantities, such as temperature, wind direction and speed, and precipitation.*
- *Water, which covers the majority of the earth's surface, circulates through the crust, oceans, and atmosphere in what is known as the "water cycle." Water evaporates from the earth's surface, rises and cools as it moves to higher elevations, condenses as rain or snow, and falls to the surface where it collects in lakes, oceans, soil, and in rocks underground.*
- *Clouds, formed by the condensation of water vapor, affect weather and climate.*

Science and Technology
- *Tools help scientists make better observations, measurements, and equipment for investigations. They help scientists see, measure, and do things that they could not otherwise see, measure, and do.*

Science in Personal and Social Perspectives
- *Safety and security are basic needs of humans. Safety involves freedom from danger, risk, or injury. Security involves feelings of confidence and lack of anxiety and fear. Student understandings include following safety rules for home and school, preventing abuse and neglect, avoiding injury, knowing whom to ask for help, and when and how to say no.*

* National Research Council. *National Science Education Standards.* National Academy Press. Washington D.C. 1996.

Project 2061 Benchmarks*

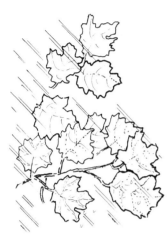

The Nature of Science
- *Scientists do not pay much attention to claims about how something they know about works unless the claims are backed up with evidence that can be confirmed and with a logical argument.*

The Nature of Technology
- *Measuring instruments can be used to gather accurate information for making scientific comparisons of objects and events and for designing and constructing things that will work properly.*

The Physical Setting
- *The sun warms the land, air, and water.*
- *When liquid water disappears, it turns into a gas (vapor) in the air and can reappear as a liquid when cooled, or as a solid if cooled below the freezing point of water.*

The Mathematical World
- *When people care about what is being counted or measured, it is important for them to say what the units are (three degrees Fahrenheit is different from three centimeters, three miles from three miles per hour).*
- *Tables and graphs can show how values of one quantity are related to values of another.*
- *Length can be thought of as unit lengths joined together, area as a collection of unit squares, and volume as a set of unit cubes.*
- *If 0 and 1 are located on a line, any other number can be depicted as a position on the line.*
- *Graphical display of numbers may make it possible to spot patterns that are not otherwise obvious, such as comparative size and trends.*
- *Many objects can be described in terms of simple plane figures and solids. Shapes can be compared in terms of concepts such as parallel and perpendicular, congruence and similarity, and symmetry. Symmetry can be found by reflection, turns, or slides.*
- *Areas of irregular shapes can be found by dividing them into squares and triangles.*

Common Themes
- *Geometric figures, number sequences, graphs, diagrams, sketches, number lines, maps, and stories can be used to represent objects, events, and processes in the real world, although such representations can never be exact in every detail.*
- *Things change in steady, repetitive, or irregular ways—or sometimes in more than one way at the same time. Often the best way to tell which kinds of change are happening is to make a table or graph of measurements.*

Habits of Mind
- *Keep records of their investigations and observations and not change the records later.*
- *Use fractions and decimals, translating when necessary between decimals and commonly encountered fractions—halves, thirds, fourths, fifths, tenths, and hundredths (but not sixths, sevenths, etc.).*
- *Keep a notebook that describes observations made, carefully distinguishes actual observations from ideas and speculations about what was observed, and is understandable weeks or months later.*
- *Use numerical data in describing and comparing objects and events.*
- *Buttress their statements with facts found in books, articles, and databases, and identify the sources used and expect others to do the same.*
- *Recognize when comparisons might not be fair because some conditions are not kept the same.*

* American Association for the Advancement of Science. *Benchmarks for Science Literacy.* Oxford University Press. New York. 1993.

NCTM Standards 2000*

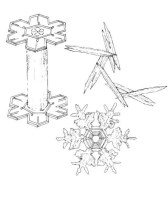

Numbers and Operations
- *Explore numbers less than 0 by extending the number line and through familiar applications*
- *Understand the place-value structure of the base-ten number system and be able to represent and compare whole numbers and decimals*

Algebra
- *Describe, extend, and make generalizations about geometric and numeric patterns*

Geometry
- *Identify, compare, and analyze attributes of two- and three-dimensional shapes and develop vocabulary to describe the attributes*
- *Recognize geometric shapes and structures in the environment and specify their location*
- *Identify and describe line and rotational symmetry in two- and three-dimensional shapes and designs*

Measurement
- *Understand the need for measuring with standard units and become familiar with standard units in the customary and metric systems*
- *Understand such attributes as length, area, weight, volume, and size of angle and select the appropriate type of unit for measuring each attribute*
- *Understand that measurements are approximations and understand how differences in units affect precision*
- *Select and apply appropriate standard units and tools to measure length, area, volume, weight, time, temperature, and the size of angles*
- *Select and use benchmarks to estimate measurements*
- *Develop strategies for estimating the perimeters, areas, and volumes of irregular shapes*

Data Analysis and Probability
- *Collect data using observations, surveys, and experiments*
- *Design investigations to address a question and consider how data-collection methods affect the nature of the data set*
- *Represent data using tables and graphs such as line plots, bar graphs, and line graphs*
- *Describe the shape and important features of a set of data and compare related data sets, with an emphasis on how the data are distributed*
- *Use measures of center, focusing on the median, and understand what each does and does not indicate about the data set*
- *Propose and justify conclusions and predictions that are based on data and design studies to further investigate the conclusions or predictions*
- *Describe events as likely or unlikely and discuss the degree of likelihood using such words as* certain, equally likely, *and* impossible

Connections
- *Recognize and apply mathematics in contexts outside of mathematics*

Representation
- *Use representations to model and interpret physical, social, and mathematical phenomena*

* Reprinted with permission from *Principles and Standards for School Mathematics*, 2000 by the National Council of Teachers of Mathematics. All rights reserved.

Management Overview

A Suggested Plan

The study of weather is too complex to be accomplished in a couple of weeks; it involves much more than taking a few measurements or addressing a few highlights. Students deserve the opportunity to study weather in depth—to look for evidence of change, to become proficient with different measuring tools, to grasp the variables involved, to acquire a greater appreciation of our world—and that requires learning over time.

As such, consider studying weather over the course of the year. Rather than to present the entire unit at one time, one suggestion is to introduce weather at the beginning of the year, then intersperse other curricular units with the various weather topics as shown below. Have students continue to gather weather data at a regular time each day throughout the year.

		Station Model
Month 1	• Throughout your Weather Studies • Temperature	Start with: • sky cover • present weather • temperature
Month 2	• Air	Add: • barometric tendency • barometric pressure
Month 3	• Wind	Add: • wind direction • wind speed
Month 4		
Month 5	• Moisture	Add: • precipitation

Assessment

Presenting opportunities for children to become actively engaged in learning is not enough. What do children know and what are they able to do? What naive conceptions are still held about the subject at hand? Which process skills have been mastered and which continue to be troublesome? One of the purposes of assessment is to inform instruction in order to more effectively meet the specific needs of your students. Layers of assessment are offered in *Weather Sense*.

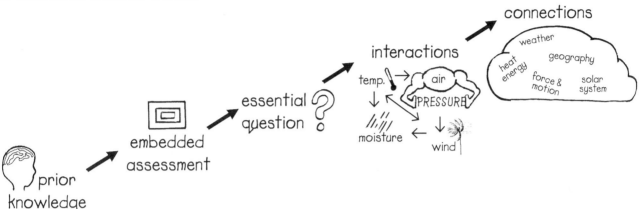

Constructing and assessing knowledge

Assessment of prior knowledge

Before embarking on any topic, it makes sense to find out what students already know. "Weather" is a rather broad subject for this task. Instead, invite students to respond to "temperature" as you prepare to study that weather element, then later to "air," "wind," and "moisture." The KWL acronym can be a helpful format for framing learning.

Things we think we know	Things we would like to know	Things we learned

Embedded assessment

Another layer is the embedded assessment which happens within an activity. Through observation of the degree of engagement, through observation of process skills being used, through questioning, and through listening to student conversations with each other, teachers are constantly assessing acquisition of concepts and skills and adapting the flow of the activity accordingly. Puzzlement about a procedure and certain conceptual questions can be dealt with immediately. Other questions may be more appropriately deferred until more knowledge has been acquired, but should be given value by being added to a class list. These observations may be informal or they may be more formally noted in an observation log. The intent of the log may be to evaluate *conceptual understanding* or it may be to assess *values, attitudes, and skills*, sometimes referred to as habits of mind.

Some activities incorporate a performance assessment within them. *A Matter of Degrees,* for example, checks progress in interpreting scales. Others, such as *Going, Going, Gone!* and *Proverb Proofs,* can be used as performance assessments if students have had sufficient prior experiences in controlling variables and designing an investigation.

Essential question

Weather Sense, in two companion publications, is built around the four fundamental elements of weather: temperature, air pressure, wind, and moisture. Each of these elements has a corresponding essential question, a question that addresses the conceptual focus of that unit. These questions are featured in the Table of Contents and on the assessment pages. When the study of a weather element commences, display the appropriate essential question in the room. As each activity comes to a close, what has been learned that day should be related back to the essential question. The goal is for specific learning to be connected to the bigger picture.

Within each weather section is also an assessment which more formally addresses the essential question or big idea. Sometimes the assessment is in the form of suggestions and sometimes it is supported by pages that can be copied.

Journals and/or portfolios are another way for students to demonstrate their thinking and learning as is mind mapping *, a visual/symbolic concept map. Also consider having students do a self-assessment, such as the partial example below, based on items you have devised.

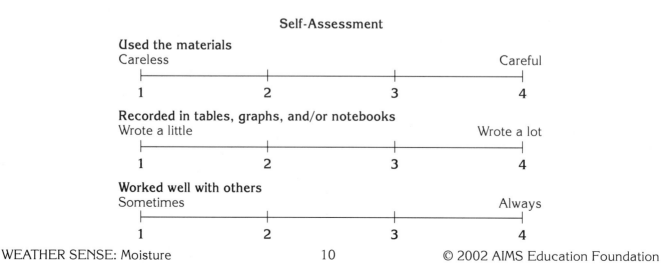

Self-Assessment

Used the materials
Careless   Careful
1   2   3   4

Recorded in tables, graphs, and/or notebooks
Wrote a little   Wrote a lot
1   2   3   4

Worked well with others
Sometimes   Always
1   2   3   4

Interactions

At the next level of conceptual development, the goal is for students to understand how one element of weather interacts with another. Some of the activity questions begin to probe these connections on an observational level, but there is no formal assessment here since students are just beginning to construct these connections.

Connections

Eventually students should understand the connections between weather and the other sciences—the solar system (earth science), heat energy and force and motion (physical science)—as well as geography. This does not happen in one year. The conceptual seeds that are planted as a result of doing these activities will make this goal more possible as students move through middle school, high school, and even college. Students are on a learning journey; it is constructive; it is developmental. We may never see the resulting fruit, but we will know we had a part in its growth.

Journals

A journal is a useful method for personal communication between teacher and student as well as a tool for assessing learning progress. From the standpoint of integrating the curriculum, the weather activities give a meaningful context for writing and illustration. A journal cover, near the front of this book, can be copied for student use. Suggestions for the journal include:

Visual	Written
diagram	response to a prompt or question
picture	description of a weather event
table/graph	comparison of two objects or events
map	interview
mind map*	composition of an original poem
	description of a walk on a ____ day
	(hot, windy, rainy, etc.)
	response to a non-fiction/fiction weather book

If you wish for students to have a hybrid mix of journal and portfolio, have them construct a folder. Include both journal entries and selected activity pages showing data collection, graphing, and descriptions of weather patterns.

* Margulies, Nancy. *Mapping Inner Space: Learning and Teaching Mind Mapping.* Zephyr Press. Tucson, AZ. 1991.

Metric or Not?

The standard used by most of the world and of scientists—and you and your class are practicing scientists—is the metric system. This includes the National Weather Service meteorologists (U.S.), although they presently report data in customary units. If at all possible, you are encouraged to obtain equipment and make measurements in metric units.

If metric measuring tools are not available, use those you have. Students should not be asked to convert from one system to the other. Records and graphs should reflect the system with which measurements were made. However, on those rare occasions when student measurements are going to be directly compared with official meteorological measurements, such as in *Temperature Tally,* use the corresponding units of measurement.

A Word about Weather Stations

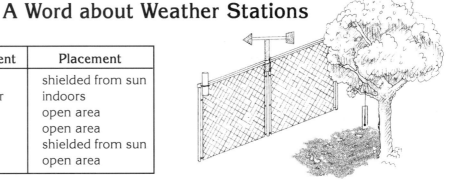

Weather Station Instrument	Placement
thermometer	shielded from sun
balloon/aneroid barometer	indoors
wind vane	open area
anemometer	open area
sling psychrometer	shielded from sun
rain gauge	open area

As the activities in these books are explored, several homemade weather instruments will be constructed. These include a balloon barometer for detecting air pressure changes, a wind vane for wind direction, an anemometer to measure wind speed, a sling psychrometer for relative humidity, and a rain gauge. These instruments, along with a thermometer, are intended to be taken outdoors at specified times and returned indoors after measurements are completed. The exceptions are the barometer, which requires the more controlled environment found indoors, and the rain gauge, which will need to stay outside for the duration of a storm.

A permanent weather station with homemade instruments is not generally feasible at a school site for several reasons. First, the homemade instruments are more fragile than commercial ones and may not be sturdy enough to withstand the variations of weather day in and day out. Second, they would need to be set up in an open area away from buildings and trees. This can be problematic since the school playground is used for so many activities and often by the community after hours. Third, to protect the thermometer from the sun, a Stevenson screen would need to be built. This box is made of wood, has vents, and is painted white, along with other specifications. A cardboard version would disintegrate in wet weather.

If you are keenly interested in a permanent weather station, commercial ones are available. Sometimes local television stations are willing to offer help in financing this effort, with an eye toward using your weather data—in addition to their own sources. Also contact community groups for financial support.

I Hear and I Forget,

I See and
I Remember,

I Do
and I
Understand.

Chinese Proverb

Weather Journal

Global Weather Extremes

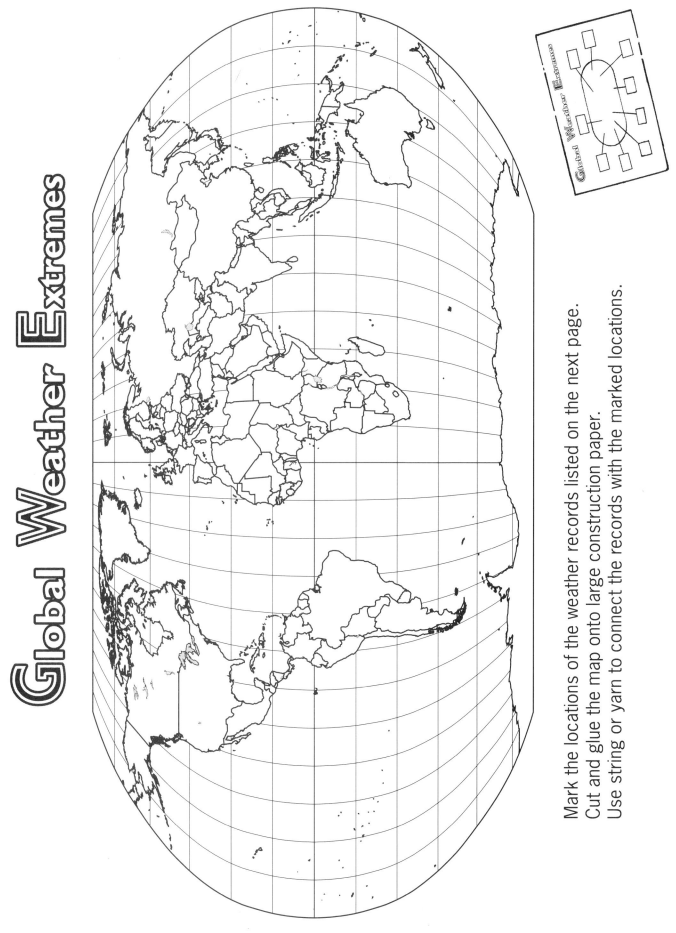

Mark the locations of the weather records listed on the next page.
Cut and glue the map onto large construction paper.
Use string or yarn to connect the records with the marked locations.

Global Weather Extremes

Use some or all of these records on the map.

Highest Temperature
58°C (136°F)
El Azizia, Libya (32°N 13°E)
September 13, 1922

Lowest Temperature
-89°C (-129°F)
Vostok, Antarctica (72°S 13°E)
July 21, 1983

Highest Air Pressure
1084 mb (32 in)
Agata, Siberia, Russia
(66°N 92°E)
December 31, 1968

Lowest Air Pressure
868 mb (25.63 in)
Typhoon Tip
(17°N 138°E, Pacific Ocean)
October 12, 1979

Highest Wind Gust
(directly measured)
372 km/h (231 mph)
Mt. Washington, New Hampshire
April 12, 1934

Highest Wind Gust
(remotely measured)
512 km/h (318 mph)
F5 tornado in Moore, Oklahoma
(suburb of Oklahoma City)
May 3, 1999

Highest Annual Average Rainfall
1187.2 cm (467.4 in)
Mawsynram, India (25°N 91°E)
(38-year span)

1168.4 cm (460.0 in)
Mt. Waialeale, Kauai, Hawaii
(32-year span)

Either of these may have the record, depending on
measurement practices and period of record variations.

Lowest Annual Average Rainfall
0.08 cm (0.03 in)
Arica, Chile (18°S 69°W)
(59-year span)

Highest Annual Total Rainfall
2644 cm (1041 in)
Cherrapunji, India (25°N 91°E)
August 1860-July 1861

Highest 24-hour Rainfall
187 cm (73.62 in)
Cilaos, Reunion Island
(21°S 56°E, South Indian Ocean)
March 15-16, 1952

Highest Annual Snowfall
289.6 cm (1140 in)
Mt. Baker, Washington
1998-1999

A Matter of DEGREES

Topic
Measurement: reading weather instrument scales

Key Question
How can we measure more precisely?

Focus
Students will determine the number patterns on a variety of scales (number lines), then apply this knowledge to measuring and graphing assorted temperatures. A different scale (barometer) will be used for assessment.

Guiding Documents
Project 2061 Benchmarks
- *Measuring instruments can be used to gather accurate information for making scientific comparisons of objects and events and for designing and constructing things that will work properly.*
- *In some situations, "0" means none of something, but in others it may be just the label of some point on a scale.*
- *If 0 and 1 are located on a line, any other number can be depicted as a position on the line.*
- *When people care about what is being counted or measured, it is important for them to say what the units are (three degrees Fahrenheit is different from three centimeters, three miles from three miles per hour).*

NRC Standard
- *Tools help scientists make better observations, measurements, and equipment for investigations. They help scientists see, measure, and do things that they could not otherwise see, measure, and do.*

NCTM Standards 2000*
- *Explore numbers less than 0 by extending the number line and through familiar applications*
- *Describe, extend, and make generalizations about geometric and numeric patterns*
- *Understand the need for measuring with standard units and become familiar with standard units in the customary and metric systems*
- *Understand that measurements are approximations and understand how differences in units affect precision*
- *Collect data using observations, surveys, and experiments*

Math
Number patterns
Estimation
Measurement
  temperature
Bar graph

Science
Earth science
  meteorology

Integrated Processes
Observing
Collecting and recording data
Comparing and contrasting
Applying

Materials
12" x 18" construction paper, 1 white and 1 red
  (see *Management 1*)
Glue
Several thermometers
Transparencies (see *Management 2*)
Toothpicks
Scissors, optional

Background Information
Procedures for precise measurement
  Scales, a practical application of the number line, are the basis of many of the measuring tools that we encounter in our daily lives—from speedometers, to rulers, to thermometers. *Since the increments on scales vary, they need to be determined.* Many, such as a thermometer, are marked in 1- or 2-unit intervals. Others, like a graduated cylinder, may jump by fives, twenties, or even hundreds. Still others are marked with parts of a whole unit (decimals), such as a rain gauge in inches; this may be because the chosen unit is large and/or very small quantities need to be measured.

  To gather meaningful data, the *unit of measurement must be identified* and labeled. This unit is usually derived from one of two measuring systems, customary or metric. Thermometers may have a Celsius or Fahrenheit scale. A rain gauge scale may be in millimeters or inches. Even more unit choices are associated with barometers: centimeters, inches, millibars, or kilopascals.

Another procedure leading toward more precise measurement is to *read the scale at eye level,* in other words, with eyes perpendicular to the measuring device. Angles other than perpendicular result in a distorted observation.

Measurement readings benefit from *careful, rather than hurried, observation of the indicator, level of liquid, etc.* Sometimes a measuring instrument, such as a thermometer, also needs to be given time to register the conditions which it is measuring before a useful reading can be taken.

The need for precise measuring skills crosses through many disciplines of mathematics and science. A study of scale also connects to graphing, both in construction, where the increment chosen has a direct effect on the way the data look, and in interpretation of data, which is dependent on recognizing the increments being used. Yet students are often not taught, or are assumed to have already acquired, the necessary skills. Determine the prior knowledge of students in evaluating whether to proceed.

Approximation of measurement

Measurements are approximate for at least three reasons. 1) Any measuring unit can be subdivided into still smaller units which are more precise. A millimeter scale is more precise than a centimeter scale. But millimeters can be further divided into tenths and those tenths can be divided into tenths and so on. 2) A measurement reading is somewhat subjective, in that the observer estimates the indicator's placement in relation to a scale; it may not be exactly at one of the scale lines. The greater the jump between increments, the more challenging the estimation becomes. Rounding to a specified unit, whether a degree or a centimeter, also results in an approximation. The larger the unit, the greater the approximation. 3) The quality and accuracy of measuring instruments vary. The measuring instruments research scientists use are more accurately callibrated and more sensitive to minute changes than the inexpensive tools generally available in schools.

Weather instruments

Scales abound in weather instruments. In the *Weather Sense* books, a thermometer will be used to measure temperature, a barometer for air pressure, a protractor and chart for wind speed, a rain gauge for rainfall totals, and a sling psychrometer with wet- and dry-bulb thermometers for relative humidity. The use of metric units is recommended in most activities, as it is the language of scientists and most of the world. Although the National Weather Service in the United States still reports temperature in degrees Fahrenheit, their measurements are taken in degrees Celsius (in conformance with international meteorological standards) and then converted.

Management

1. To make the thermometer bands, cut the construction paper into six-inch widths. Glue a red sheet to a white sheet, overlapping about $\frac{1}{2}$ inch along the 18-inch edges. When dry, cut into $\frac{1}{4}$-inch widths. Each student will need one band.

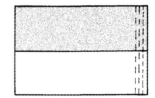

2. Transparencies of the activity pages, used on the overhead projector, are helpful for instructing about scales, modeling thermometer procedure, and for showing data results. To make a transparent thermometer band, cut a $\frac{1}{4}$-inch strip from the edge of the transparency and color half of it with a red marker.

3. This activity has three parts: practice in identifying and numbering scales, hands-on experience with a thermometer, and assessment with a barometer scale. Use the thermometer page (1- or 2-degree increments) that corresponds to your thermometers.

4. Before distributing the thermometer page, make the slits for the thermometer band with a craft knife or razor blade. Also cut slits in the matching transparency. Alternatively, students can fold the line to be slit in half and make small cuts with scissors.

5. Decide which temperature measurements will be taken. They do not need to relate to weather. Indoor examples include placing the thermometer in the center of the room, on a window ledge, inside a desk, on the floor, near the ceiling, in ice water, in hot water, or with a hand closed around the bulb.

6. If measuring in degrees Celsius, display the *Celsius Poem* so students can begin to relate common temperatures with the numbers. Water boils at 100°C and freezes at 0°C. Normal body temperature is 37°.

Procedure

Scale savvy

1. On the chalkboard or a transparency, draw the following scale:

   Ask, "What is this scale counting by?" [ones] "What numbers are missing?" [1, 2, 3] Add them to the scale. "Could there be smaller numbers in between, say, the 0 and the 1?" [Yes, $\frac{1}{2}$ or .5 and $\frac{1}{10}$ or .1, for example.] Explain that the smaller numbers would make the measurements, whatever the unit, even more precise.

   Erase the numbers and re-label the scale as shown:

   Ask, "What is this scale counting by?" [fives] "What numbers are missing?" [5, 10, 20] "Where would 13 be on this scale?" [between 10 and 15, but closer to 15] "If you were graphing using this scale, what could help you more carefully choose where 13 should be? [marking the distance between 10 and 15 into five equal spaces]

   Because scales vary, inform students that any time they use a measuring tool, they need to identify the measuring unit and the jumps, or increments, on the scale.

2. Give students the first activity page and have them record the following numbers as shown:

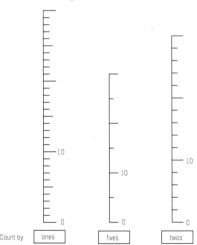

Count by	ones	fives	twos

3. Direct the students' attention to the first scale. Ask, "How many marked spaces are between 1 and 10?" [10] "So each line jumps by how much?" [1] Have them write in the amount of the jump as well as the missing numbers (or at least the fives)

on the scale. Ask students to point to where 17 would be on the scale, then 6. Continue in the same manner with the other scales. "On which scale(s) was it easiest to find 17?" [probably the first scale] "How about 6?" [both the first and the third scales] "Which scale is most precise?" [the first one]

Depending on your curricular goals, another copy of this page can be used for practicing with negative numbers, decimals, and/or larger increments.

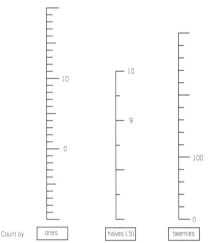

Count by	ones	halves (.5)	twenties

negative numbers   decimals   larger increments

4. Encourage students to hunt for a variety of scales in the classroom and at home. See the journal prompt at the end of *Discussion*.

Hands on experience: thermometers

1. Distribute the chosen temperature page, thermometer bands, and thermometers. Have students number both the thermometer and the graph scales at the longest lines only (tens). If Celsius is being used, the scale should start at -20° and go to 100°. For Fahrenheit, pick a range that will encompass the temperatures that students will take.

2. Instruct students about the procedures for taking precise measurements (see *Background Information*). Additional precautions specific to thermometers include keeping hands away from the bulb and reading the thermometer before removing it from the environment being measured.

   Have small groups measure the room's air temperature, slide their temperature bands through the slits, and position them to reflect their readings.

3. Share results as you walk around observing the thermometers and assessing the use of the scale. The thermometer band can be quickly repositioned, if necessary, leaving no record of mistakes.

Discuss possible reasons for temperature variations by asking, "Why might our thermometers give different measurements?" [They didn't match to start with, one place in the room might be cooler than another, they weren't read carefully, etc.] Give further instruction as needed and direct students to complete the first column of the temperature graph.

4. Encourage students to suggest (or you choose) four more temperature-taking experiences. Each measurement should be shown with the thermometer band and recorded on the graph. Completed graphs should have three labels: the title, the measuring unit (°C or °F), and the names of the five things that were measured.

5. As students engage in temperature measurement, assess their use of specific procedures for taking precise measurements: waiting for the thermometer to register the temperature, reading the scale at eye level, interpreting the scale correctly, and identifying the measurement unit (°C or °F).

Scale assessment

1. Have each student use the barometer page and a toothpick as an indicator to show measurements you say, such as 1018 millibars, 1007 millibars, and so on. The curved path provides a new twist, and the presence of two scales puts students' interpretation skills to the test. Success depends on attention to the appropriate measuring unit and identification of the scale increments.

2. Use the inch scale for additional experiences, if desired.

Discussion

1. Which is easier to read, a scale that jumps by ones or a scale that jumps by twos? [a scale that jumps by ones] Why? [You estimate more when a scale jumps by twos because some of the counting numbers are missing.]

2. Why don't all scales jump by ones? [There may not be enough room for all the lines, bigger jumps are needed when dealing with larger numbers, etc.]

3. How is *zero* on a temperature scale different from *zero* pieces of pie? [For temperature, *zero* is a label of a point on the scale but when counting pies, it means you have none.]

4. Why is it important to name the unit with which you are measuring? [Different units have different meanings. For example, 20° Celsius means the temperature is comfortable, but 20° Fahrenheit means it is colder than freezing.] What does *zero* mean on the Celsius scale? [freezing point of water] ...on the Fahrenheit scale? [colder than the freezing point of water]

5. How do the Fahrenheit and Celsius scales compare? [may have different increments, the units are not the same because the numbers across from each other don't match—10 in °C is 50 in °F]

6. Does the temperature of what you are measuring change when you switch from Celsius to Fahrenheit? [No, the temperature physically remains the same. It is just being measured by different units of heat energy.]

7. Where have you seen Celsius temperatures reported? [time and temperature signs on businesses, international weather websites, etc.]

8. Give an example of how measurement is approximate.

 Journal Prompt: Find and record as many measuring tools with scales as possible. List the measuring unit and by how much they jump. An example:

Tool	Increment	Unit
ruler	16ths	inches
ruler	10ths	centimeters
thermometer	2	degrees Celsius
thermometer	1	degrees Fahrenheit
barometer	2	millibars
barometer	20ths	inches
protractor	1	degrees
graduated cylinder	1	milliliters
spring scale	10	grams
spring scale	1	newtons
speedometer	10	miles per hour
speedometer	20	kilometers per hour
bathroom scale	1	pounds/kilograms

* Reprinted with permission from *Principles and Standards for School Mathematics*, 2000 by the National Council of Teachers of Mathematics. All rights reserved.

A Matter of DEGREES

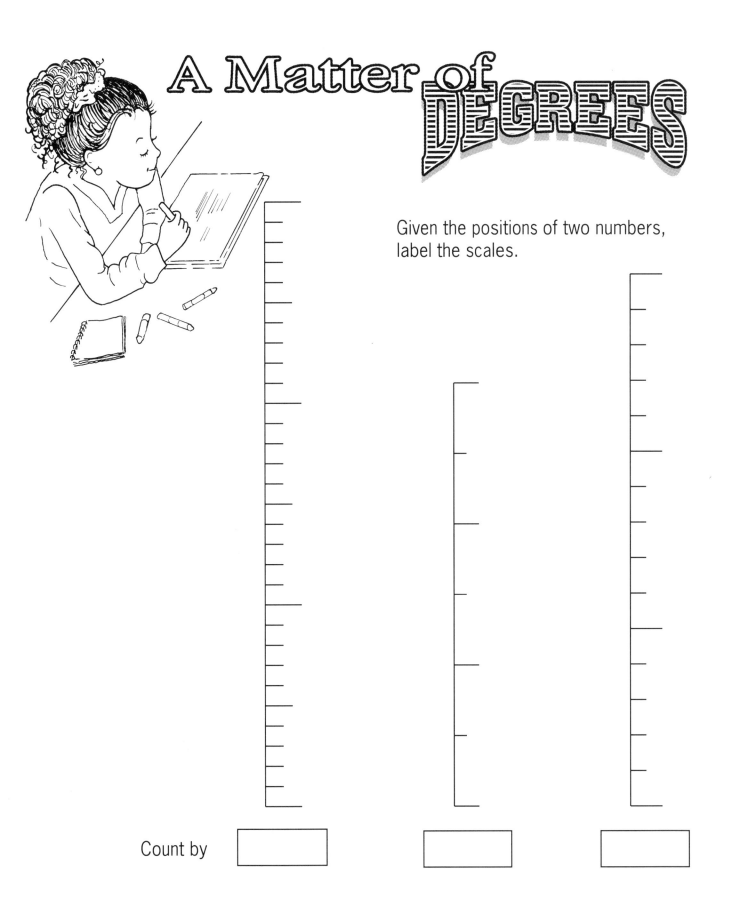

Given the positions of two numbers, label the scales.

Count by [ ]

What kinds of scales can you find?
How are they divided?
What units of measurement do they use?

• Wait until the thermometer liquid stops moving.
• Read at eye level.
• Record to the nearest degree.

Show the temperature with
your thermometer band.

Temperature Graph

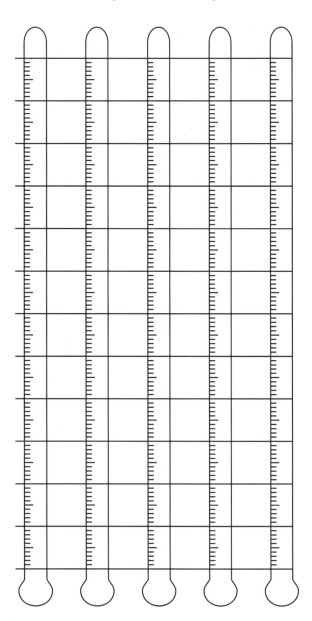

A Matter of

- Wait until the thermometer liquid stops moving.
- Read at eye level.
- Record to the nearest degree.

Show the temperature with your thermometer band.

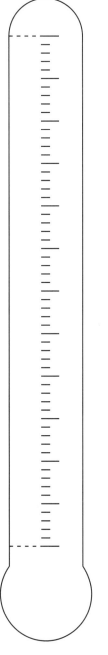

Temperature Graph

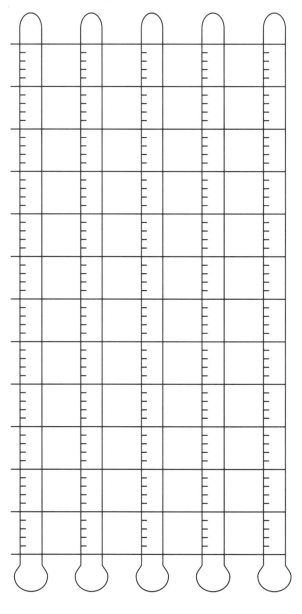

A Matter of DEGREES

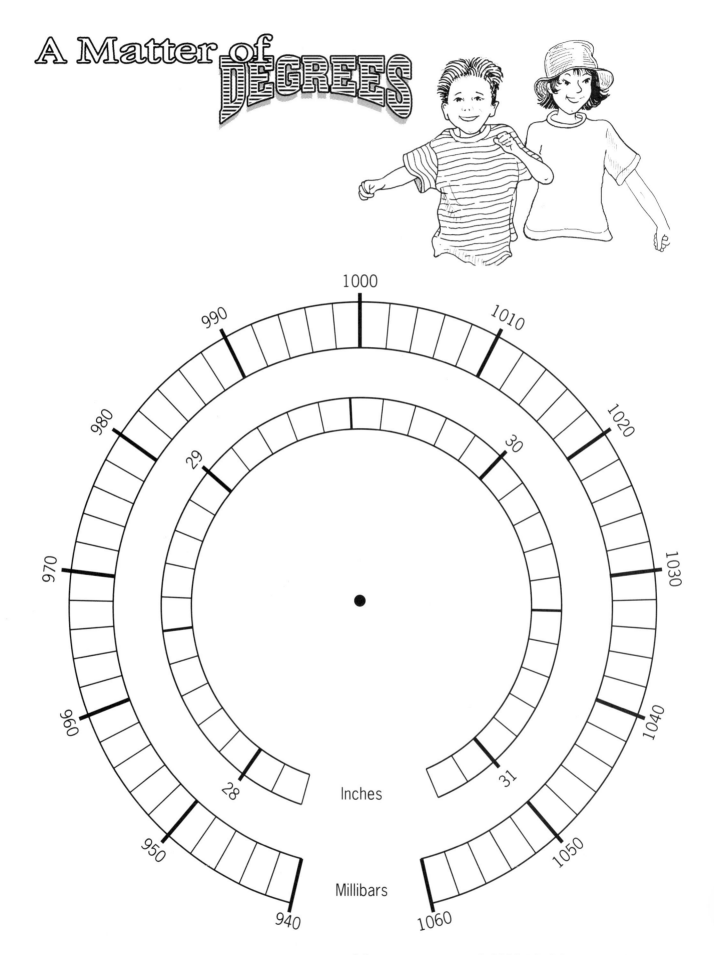

1000

990

1010

980

1020

970

1030

960

1040

950

1060

940

29

30

28

31

Inches

Millibars

Proverb Proofs

Topic
Weather proverbs

Challenge
Design an investigation to test one of the weather proverbs.

Focus
Each student group will choose a weather proverb, make a plan to test its accuracy, gather data, and report conclusions.

Guiding Documents
Project 2061 Benchmarks
- *Scientific investigations may take many different forms, including observing what things are like or what is happening somewhere, collecting specimens for analysis, and doing experiments. Investigations can focus on physical, biological, and social questions.*
- *Keep a notebook that describes observations made, carefully distinguishes actual observations from ideas and speculations about what was observed, and is understandable weeks or months later.*

NRC Standards
- *Plan and conduct a simple investigation.*
- *Employ simple equipment and tools to gather data and extend the senses.*
- *Communicate investigations and explanations.*

NCTM Standards 2000*
- *Design investigations to address a question and consider how data-collection methods affect the nature of the data set*
- *Collect data using observations, surveys, and experiments*
- *Represent data using tables and graphs such as line plots, bar graphs, and line graphs*

Math (dependent on proverbs chosen and student plans)
Measurement
Graphing
Statistics

Science
Earth science
    meteorology
Scientific inquiry

Integrated Processes
Observing
Predicting
Collecting and recording data
Comparing and contrasting
Interpreting data
Relating

Materials
Dependent on student plans

Background Information
Throughout history, people in outdoor occupations such as farming, fishing, or sheepherding were very aware of the weather because it directly affected their work. They looked for patterns—in the sky, in plant and animal life, and in their own bodies—that would help predict the weather. These observations became sayings or proverbs, often given in easy-to-remember verse. Weather proverbs are found in many different cultures, although the ones presented in this book are predominantly from the United States and Europe.

Some proverbs are based on solid science, others have a grain of truth in them (valid at times or in certain locations), and some are false. An example of the latter: Thunder curdles cream or lightning sours milk. As a National Oceanic and Atmospheric Administration (NOAA) publication states, "The trouble with weather proverbs is not so much that they're all wrong, but that they're not all right for all times in all places."[1] This makes proverbs ripe for testing using the scientific process.

Students can make predictions, decide what kind of data need to be collected and how much data is enough to draw a conclusion, and communicate their results. They may need to watch the sky or the behavior of a particular plant or animal as well as the current weather conditions or those which follow. A study of weather proverbs blends together history, language arts, science, and math.

1. National Oceanic and Atmospheric Administration. *The Amateur Weather Forecaster.* Vol. 9, Number 4. October 1979. (NOAA reprint of "Weather Proverbs by R.E. Spencer, formerly of the National Weather Service, first published in the December 27, 1954 issue of the *Weekly Weather and Crop Bulletin.*)

Management
1. Weather proverbs are presented near the beginning of each of the four major sections of *Weather Sense*—temperature, air pressure, wind, and moisture. You are encouraged to use this process and activity page each time you begin a study of a new weather element.

2. This activity will be done over a period of time. Allow at least one day for students to gather weather proverbs from their families (the first time only), another day to choose a proverb and design a plan to test it, a period of time—possibly several weeks—in which to gather data, and then further time to organize and report their results.

3. Each group of students will need to design a plan first in order to know what materials will need to be gathered.

The following is offered for those students ready for more independent work.

> *Open-ended:* Issue the *Challenge* and, without the guidance of leading questions, encourage each student group to devise a plan for testing a proverb.

Procedure
First time

1. Have students ask their parents, grandparents, or family friends about weather sayings they have heard. Record their findings on a class chart that can be on view throughout their weather study.

2. Explain that before weather instruments were invented, people—particularly farmers, shepherds, sailors, and others who worked outdoors—would observe the skies, animals, and plants around them for signs of changing weather. Over time, people developed sayings or proverbs based on their observations.

   Tell students that they will be examining some of these proverbs and then pick one to test for its truthfulness or accuracy.

Each time

1. Give each group one of the proverbs pages—temperature, air pressure, wind, or moisture—or study the list of collected proverbs.

2. Distribute the planning page. Have each group choose a proverb and use the planning page to design the investigation.

3. Gather the necessary materials and instruct students to implement their plans.

4. Allow sufficient time for groups to organize and present their data and conclusions. Encourage them to make a drawing illustrating their proverb.

5. Repeat this activity when another weather element is presented.

Discussion

1. What kinds of jobs are most affected by weather? [construction workers, pilots, farmers, ranchers, fishermen, taxicab drivers, etc.]

2. What was the most difficult part about testing the proverb you chose?

3. How accurate (true) is the proverb you chose? Do you feel you have gathered enough data to be sure of your conclusion? Why or why not?

4. What further questions do you have as a result of your test?

Teacher Resources
Davis, Hubert. *A January Fog Will Freeze a Hog.* Crown Publishers. New York. 1977. (currently out of print but may be found in a library)

Dolan, Edward F. *The Old Farmer's Almanac Book of Weather Lore.* Ivy Books (Ballantine). New York. 1988.

Freier, George D. *Weather Proverbs.* Fisher Books. Tucson, AZ. 1989.

Jones, M. Gail and Glenda Carter. "Weather Folklore: Fact or Fiction?" *Science and Children.* September, 1995. (Gives examples of how specific weather proverbs were tested by students.)

Lee, Albert. *Weather Wisdom.* Doubleday. Garden City, NY. 1976. (out of print)

Lockhart, Gary. *The Weather Companion.* John Wiley & Sons, Inc. New York. 1988.

Sloane, Eric. *Folklore of American Weather.* Duell, Sloan and Pearce. New York. 1963. (currently out of print)

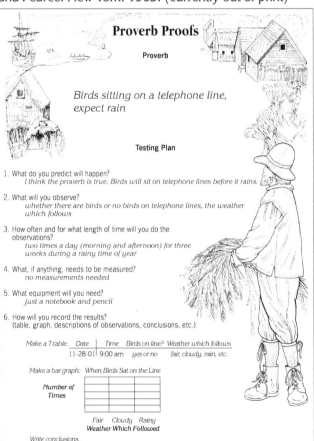

Proverb Proofs

Proverb

Birds sitting on a telephone line, expect rain

Testing Plan

1. What do you predict will happen?
   I think the proverb is true. Birds will sit on telephone lines before it rains.

2. What will you observe?
   whether there are birds or no birds on telephone lines, the weather which follows

3. How often and for what length of time will you do the observations?
   two times a day (morning and afternoon) for three weeks during a rainy time of year

4. What, if anything, needs to be measured?
   no measurements needed

5. What equipment will you need?
   just a notebook and pencil

6. How will you record the results?
   (table, graph, descriptions of observations, conclusions, etc.)

   Make a T-table: Date | Time | Birds on line? | Weather which follows
   11-28-01 | 9:00 am | yes or no | fair, cloudy, rain, etc.

   Make a bar graph: When Birds Sat on the Line

   Number of Times

   Fair   Cloudy   Rainy
   Weather Which Followed

   Write conclusions.

Performance Assessment

For older students who have had multiple prior experiences designing and carrying out investigations, this activity might be used as a performance assessment of process skills.

Learning Goals
- Identify the relevant variables to be observed
- Gather sufficient evidence to prove or disprove a proverb
- Organize and label data in a meaningful table and/or graph, diagram, etc.
- Offer a conclusion supported by the data

Evidence of Learning (Rubric)

	Variables	Evidence	Organization	Conclusion
4 Exceeds expectations	Identifies the key variable as well as time, weather, and any other relevant variable	Gathers abundant data, measured and/or anecdotal	Data is well-organized, titled, and labeled in two meaningful ways; work is neat, clear and legible	Thoughtful conclusion supported by data; creative presentation or raises a new question/hypothesis
3 Matches expectations	Identifies the relevant variables, including time and weather	Gathers a sufficient amount of data	Organizes data in at least one meaningful way, legible	States a conclusion supported by data
2 Attempts to meet expectations	Identifies some, but not all, relevant variables or includes an irrelevant variable	Amount of data is a little less than adequate	Data partially organized, labels may be incomplete	Conclusion not fully supported by data, may project opinion or expected conclusion
1 Minimal attempt to meet expectations	Identifies insufficient variables or both relevant and irrelevant variables	Obvious lack of sufficient data	Data not accurately represented, unorganized, and/or incomplete	Conclusion not supported by data or no conclusion offered

* Reprinted with permission from *Principles and Standards for School Mathematics,* 2000 by the National Council of Teachers of Mathematics. All rights reserved.

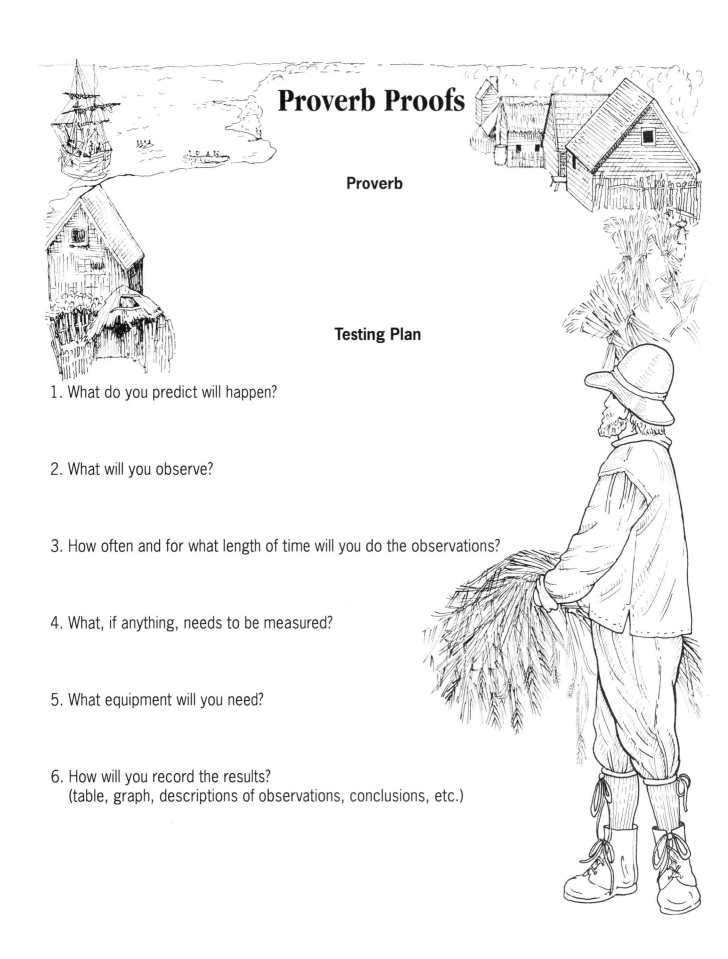

Proverb Proofs

Proverb

Testing Plan

1. What do you predict will happen?

2. What will you observe?

3. How often and for what length of time will you do the observations?

4. What, if anything, needs to be measured?

5. What equipment will you need?

6. How will you record the results?
   (table, graph, descriptions of observations, conclusions, etc.)

Station Model

Topic
Displaying weather data: graphic model

Key Questions
1. How can we show weather data at a glance?
2. How can we use current weather data to forecast the weather?

Focus
Students will learn to construct and interpret a "station model," a concise, graphic display of weather conditions used by meteorologists on surface weather maps. The station model will also be used to forecast weather.

Guiding Documents

Project 2061 Benchmarks
- *Geometric figures, number sequences, graphs, diagrams, sketches, number lines, maps, and stories can be used to represent objects, events, and processes in the real world, although such representations can never be exact in every detail.*
- *Things change in steady, repetitive, or irregular ways—or sometimes in more than one way at the same time. Often the best way to tell which kinds of change are happening is to make a table or graph of measurements.*

NRC Standards
- *Weather changes from day to day and over the seasons. Weather can be described by measurable quantities, such as temperature, wind direction and speed, and precipitation.*
- *Use appropriate tools and techniques to gather, analyze, and interpret data.*

NCTM Standards 2000*
- *Select and apply appropriate standard units and tools to measure length, area, volume, weight, time, temperature, and the size of angles*
- *Collect data using observations, surveys, and experiments*
- *Use representations to model and interpret physical, social, and mathematical phenomena*

Math
Estimation
　area (sky cover)
Measurement
　temperature
　air pressure
　angle, optional for wind speed
　depth (rain gauge)
Graphic model

Science
Earth science
　meteorology

Integrated Processes
Observing
Collecting and recording data
Comparing and contrasting
Interpreting data
Relating
Predicting

Materials
Black and white construction paper (see *Management*)
2-inch to 3-inch squares of white/pastel construction paper or sticky notes (see *Management*)
Black felt-tipped pens
Pushpins

Background Information
　A station model is a concise graphic used by meteorologists to show weather conditions for a particular location. The position of each data entry is specified as shown on the *Station Model* page. Though the station model can show a formidable amount of data, only the basic data students will be gathering are incorporated here. Several charts showing the symbols used by meteorologists are also included. There is no designated location for relative humidity on the model.

　Data from the following activities should be added to the station model as these weather elements are studied.

Sky cover:	*Sky Cover*, chart included here
Present weather:	chart included here
Temperature:	*Temperature Tally*
Barometric tendency:	*Highs and Lows*, chart included here
Barometric pressure:	*Aneroid Barometer* or *Highs and Lows*
Wind direction:	*Wind Ways*, compass rose
Wind speed:	*Just a Gust?*, chart included here
Precipitation:	*Rain Check*

This activity is both the beginning of the weather unit and the culmination. By the time students have worked their way through the various facets of weather, they will be ready to make more complete records using the table. Based on this information, some limited forecasting for the local area can be done. This lays the foundation for future, more informed forecasting through the examination of weather patterns across the country such as isotherms, isobars, high and low pressure systems, and fronts.

Management
Location
Identify a section of the bulletin board, perhaps by a yarn or paper border, for the station model. Label the model with either your city or school name. Attach data, written on construction paper squares, and symbols with pushpins.

If bulletin board space is not available, a 12" x 18" piece of laminated construction paper can provide the field for the station model. Numerical data can be written on sticky notes and symbols (sky cover and wind) attached with tape or similar means.

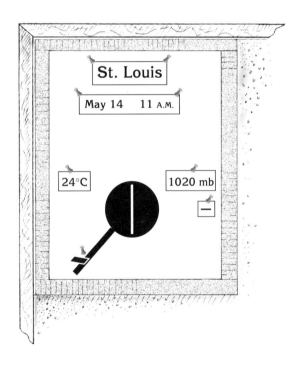

Materials
Make one copy of each symbol chart to display near the station model. Add the appropriate chart when a new weather element is introduced. Additional copies of the charts may be made for small groups or individual students, if desired.

Prepare, or have students prepare, the six sky cover symbols (black and white) and the wind symbols (black) from construction paper. The *Templates* page can be used as a guide. Assemble the wind symbols, as needed, with pushpins or tape. To extend their usefulness, consider laminating.

Time
At first, the station model will only show sky cover and present weather. Over time, as the different concepts are studied, temperature, air pressure, wind direction and speed, and precipitation will be added to the model.

Update the station model at a certain time each day or at more frequent intervals. Once started, it takes very little time for students to maintain the station model all year, even after formal weather studies have concluded.

Procedure
Introduction
1. Give students the *Station Model* page and study it together.
2. Present the *Sky Cover* chart, since sky cover is the basis around which the model is built. Take the class outside to an open area. Have students look at the entire visible sky, estimate the percentage that is covered with clouds of any kind, and choose the corresponding sky cover symbol.
3. Introduce the *Present Weather* chart. Explain that these are some of the most common symbols used to describe weather. Curious students can locate additional symbols by searching the Internet.
4. Have a student draw the proper symbol on a sticky note or small piece of paper and position it correctly on the station model. If the weather is fair, no symbol will be displayed.

After "Temperature Tally" (see AIMS book *Weather Sense: Temperature, Air Pressure, and Wind*)
Instruct students to add temperature data to the model, including °C or °F, by writing it on a sticky note or construction paper square.

After "Highs and Lows" (see AIMS book *Weather Sense: Temperature, Air Pressure, and Wind*)

Explain that the balloon barometer can indicate barometric tendency—change in the last three hours. Have students compare their current and previous data to determine whether the air pressure is rising, steady, or falling, then place the correct symbol from the barometric tendency chart on the model. Inform them that this is a key indicator of coming weather.

rising   steady   falling

Optional: Using the non-customary units on the balloon barometer's scale, instruct students to add the barometric pressure on the station model.

After "Aneroid Barometer" (see AIMS book *Weather Sense: Temperature, Air Pressure, and Wind*)

In lieu of the non-customary balloon barometer measurement, have students add the millibars (or inches) measurement of barometric pressure to the station model.

After "Wind Ways" (see AIMS book *Weather Sense: Temperature, Air Pressure, and Wind*)

Display the *Wind Direction and Speed* chart. Consult the compass rose, then model how to show the current wind direction by adding a long black bar (see *Management)* to the sky cover symbol.

After "Just a Gust?" (see AIMS book *Weather Sense: Temperature, Air Pressure, and Wind*)

Based on the data gathered, instruct students to determine the wind speed symbol needed from the chart. Have students pin or tape the appropriate barbs and/or pennants to the long bar on the station model.

After "Rain Check"

Have students record the amount of rain or melted snow on a piece of paper, labeled with millimeters or inches, and add it to the station model.

Forecasting
1. Have students keep a daily record of weather data, individually, in groups, or as a class. Students can devise their own record-keeping method or use the table in this activity. The table includes a place where small, successive versions of the station model can be drawn.
2. Instruct students to study the most current or a series of weather data, looking for a trend or pattern. Pay particular attention to the barometric tendency, wind direction, and cloud types, if clouds have been identified. Ask students to forecast

what the weather will be like in a few hours or the next day. Forecasts are more easily made if information is gathered more frequently than once a day.
3. Compare actual weather data with predicted weather. Evaluate what was learned.

Discussion
1. Look at the station model. What does it tell you? [At ____ (time), the sky was ___ (sky cover), the temperature was __, the wind was coming from the ___ (direction) at ___ (speed), and the barometer was ___ (tendency).]
2. As you study several of the most recent station models, what patterns or trends, if any, do you notice?
3. What kind of weather do you predict we will have later today or tomorrow? (Example: A rainstorm is likely.) On what did you base your prediction? (Students should refer to specific measurements on the station model. Example: The barometer is falling and we know that lower pressure can mean a storm is coming. Also, the wind is coming from the south and, in our area, that usually means rain or snow. Because the temperature is well above freezing, I think we will have rain rather than snow.)
4. Compare weather records from different seasons: How does our weather in fall compare with our weather in winter (or other seasons)?
5. Relate a country-wide weather map and your station model: How does our station model relate to the national picture of weather? (Example: There is a cold front moving in our direction and a low pressure area nearby. That explains why our barometer and the temperature are dropping and the wind is getting stronger. A storm is on the way.)

Extensions
1. Station models can also be used to show weather in other places, using data gathered from newspapers, television weather reports, and the Internet. Encourage each group to choose a city (maybe tied to history studies), locate its weather data, construct a station model, and place the model on a large map. Reduce the size of the station models so they do not obscure the map. You may wish to focus on cities in your state, across the United States, or around the world.
2. Look at surface weather maps that show partial station models on the Internet (see *Weather Websites).*

Station Model

A station model is a special way to display the weather conditions at any given location. Each piece of information belongs in a specific place. A partial station model is sometimes used on surface weather maps.

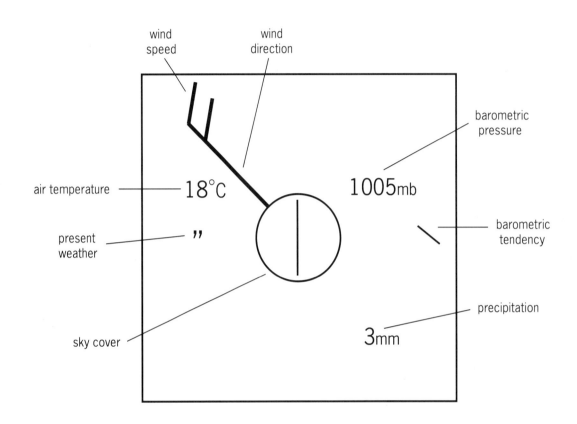

─────────────────────────── **Key** ───────────────────────────

Sky cover: see *Sky Cover* chart

Present weather: see *Present Weather* chart

Temperature: current air temperature in Celsius or Fahrenheit

Air pressure: air pressure in millibars, millimeters, or inches
Sea level normals are 1013.25 mb, 760 mm, or 29.92 inches.

Barometric tendency:
(change in past 3 hours)
rising   steady   falling

Wind direction and speed: see *Wind Direction and Speed* chart

Precipitation: rain/snow during the last 6 hours in millimeters or hundredths of an inch

Station Model

Templates

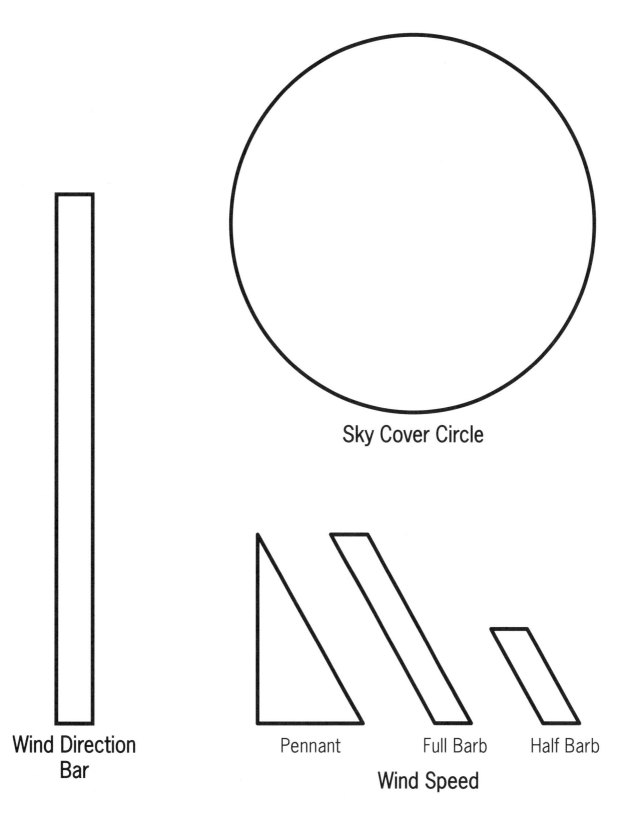

Sky Cover Circle

Wind Direction
Bar

Pennant   Full Barb   Half Barb

Wind Speed

Sky Cover

(open circle)	Clear	No clouds
(circle with vertical line)	Few	present but < 10%
(circle with one quarter filled)	Scattered	10 - 50%
(filled circle with vertical white line)	Broken	50 - 90%
(fully filled circle)	Overcast	more than 90%
(circle with X)	Obscured	**cannot be observed** (possibly fog, haze, blowing snow, smoke, volcanic ash, dust, sand, sea spray, heavy rain, or heavy snow)

Present Weather

Reduced Visibility	Drizzle	Rain	Snow	Other Precipitation	Thunderstorm	Other
smoke	slight	slight	slight	slight rain and snow	slight/moderate	lightning
haze	moderate	moderate	moderate	sleet	heavy	funnel clouds
light fog	heavy	heavy	heavy	slight hail	slight/moderate with rain	
heavy fog	slight freezing (glaze)		slight/moderate drifting	moderate/heavy hail	slight/moderate with snow	
slight/moderate dust/sandstorm					slight/moderate with hail	
severe dust/sandstorm						

Wind Direction and Speed

Wind Speed
(1 knot = 1.85 km/h or 1.15 mph)

Symbol	Knots	Kilometers per hour	Miles (Statute) per hour
◎	Calm	Calm	Calm
	1-2	1-4	1-2
	3-7	5-13	3-8
	8-12	14-23	9-14
	13-17	24-32	15-20
	18-22	33-41	21-25
	23-27	42-50	26-31
	28-32	51-60	32-37
	33-37	61-69	38-43
	38-42	70-79	44-49
	43-47	80-87	50-54
	48-52	88-97	55-60
	53-57	98-106	61-66
	58-62	107-115	67-71
	63-67	116-124	72-77
	68-72	125-134	78-83
	73-77	135-143	84-89
	103-107	190-198	119-123

Wind Direction

Use the compass rose to position the bar extending from the sky cover symbol.

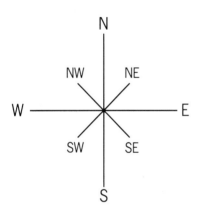

Weather Station Chart

Date/Time					
Station Model	◯	◯	◯	◯	◯
Sky Cover					
Present Weather					
Temperature					
Barometric Tendency					
Barometric Pressure					
Wind Direction and Speed					
Precipitation					

The Water Cycle

Background for the Teacher

Over time, the total amount of our world's water has not changed; it is all we will ever have. Water continually circulates between the Earth's surface, the air, and underground, changing form but not increasing or decreasing in total volume. About 97 percent of this water is the salty water found in the oceans. The other 3 percent is fresh water, most of it in glaciers and icecaps with smaller amounts underground, in rivers and lakes, and in the atmosphere.

The circulation of water is driven by heat energy from the sun. As the sun warms the surface of oceans and other water sources, the movement of water molecules quickens and some escape to become water vapor in the atmosphere. If cooled, the vapor molecules slow down and condense on tiny particles in the air and fall back to Earth as liquid or solid precipitation.

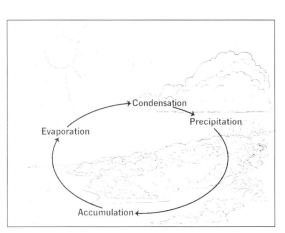

Evaporation

Molecules are always in motion. The motion is greatest in gases and slowest in solids. *It is an increase or decrease in the motion of water molecules that causes evaporation and condensation.* Heat energy increases motion. Heat energy can change a solid into a liquid (snowflake into water) and a liquid into a gas (water to water vapor). When water molecules are heated by the sun, they move more quickly until some escape the surface of the water, becoming airborne and changing to water vapor. The water vapor molecules move about in the space available between the molecules of nitrogen, oxygen, and other gases of which the air is composed.

Most water vapor, about 85%, comes from the oceans. Plants also contribute water vapor. The water drawn through their roots eventually evaporates from tiny holes on the underside of leaves in a process called transpiration. Don't underestimate their contribution to the water cycle as a full-grown tree can release as much as 40,000 gallons of water a year into the air. Water also evaporates from puddles, ponds, rivers, drying clothes, and even our skin.

Humidity

Humidity is the amount of water vapor in the air. It affects the kind of weather we may have and our degree of comfort. The amount of water vapor in the air varies with temperature; because warm air causes the motion of water molecules to quicken, more of them evaporate into the air than when the air is cold.

Relative humidity is the amount of water vapor in the air compared to the amount of water vapor that can be absorbed by the air at a given temperature. When the air can absorb no more moisture, when as many water vapor molecules are leaving (evaporation) as are changing back into water (condensation), the air is *saturated* and we say its relative humidity is 100%. Relative humidity is the percentage of saturation. It takes more water vapor to reach the saturation point in warm conditions than in cold conditions. The following chart* shows saturation levels at various temperatures. One gram is equal to one milliliter or one cubic centimeter.

Air temperature	Amount of water vapor at saturation (per cubic meter)
5°C	5.0 g
10°C	7.0 g
15°C	10.0 g
20°C	14.0 g
25°C	20.0 g
30°C	26.5 g
35°C	35.0 g
40°C	47.0 g

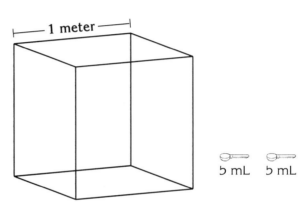

It takes 10 g or mL of water vapor to saturate one cubic meter of air at 15°C.

Condensation

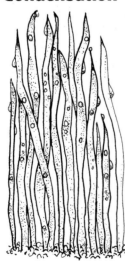

The water vapor molecules in the air are carried by the wind, often meeting changes in temperature. In a typical convection current, for example, warm, moist air rises and cools at a rate of 2.8°C for about every 300 meters (5.4°F for every 1000 feet) of altitude gain. If the air cools to the dew point temperature (which varies), the water vapor molecules slow enough to join together. In the atmosphere, these molecules condense on tiny particles—*condensation nuclei*—such as salt from sea spray, dust, smoke, volcanic ash, and pollutants, to form clouds. On Earth, water vapor may condense as dew or, if temperatures are at or below freezing (0°C or 32°F), directly into frost or ice.

* Lutgens, Frederick K. and Tarbuck, Edward J. *The Atmosphere: An Introduction to Meteorology.* Prentice Hall. Englewood Cliffs, NJ. 1989.

Precipitation

If the cloud droplets continue to gather moisture and grow large enough, gravity may overcome the buoyancy of the air and they fall back to Earth. Scientists have put forth two theories to explain the growth of raindrops, *coalescence* and the *ice crystal theory*. Coalescence happens in warm clouds, those made of water droplets. The larger droplets fall through a cloud more quickly than smaller ones. As they fall, they collide with other droplets and join together. It takes about one million cloud droplets to form a raindrop.

The formation of raindrops in cold clouds, those with ice crystals as well as water droplets, is explained by the ice crystal theory. As the combination of cloud droplets bump into each other, the water droplets attach themselves to the ice crystals. When the crystals become large enough, they descend toward Earth.

The type of precipitation that reaches the ground depends on the temperature of the air through which the crystals fall. If the air is chilly all the way down, they fall as flakes of *snow*. Snow crystal shapes vary, each group largely determined by temperature. Sometimes the crystals fall through a layer of warmer air and melt, then enter a layer of colder air and refreeze into *sleet*. If the ice crystals fall through warmer air in the lower atmosphere, they melt and become *rain*. When ice crystals are carried up and down by strong air currents in thunderclouds (cumulonimbus), *hail* can form. Hailstones often grow in layers as moisture is added during their turbulent motion.

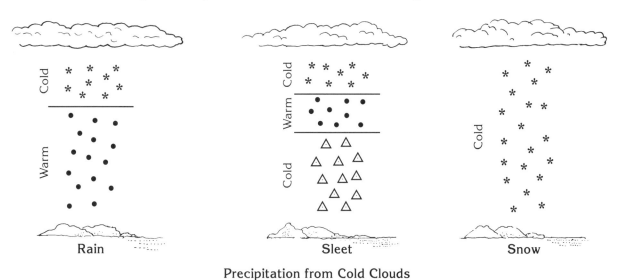

Precipitation from Cold Clouds

The amount of precipitation received on Earth varies widely. Most precipitation, over 70 percent, falls into the oceans. The amount that falls on land depends on location, elevation, and phenomena such as El Niño. Some tropical regions may receive 1000 cm (400 in) or more a year while deserts, including some polar regions, may receive less than 25 cm (10 in).

Accumulation

Whether precipitation falls as rain, snow, or ice, most of it will eventually turn into liquid water. Most precipitation falls into oceans. Of the remaining precipitation, some soaks into the tiny spaces between rocks and soil in the ground. When the ground cannot hold any more water, it collects on the surface—in small streams, marshes, and lakes. Much of this water eventually flows, drips, or seeps back to the ocean, pulled downhill by the force of gravity. Some precipitation evaporates immediately or is soaked up through the roots of plants and is later released through the leaves.

And the water cycle continues.

In Balance

The water cycle is constantly in motion. Sometimes evaporation dominates, sometimes condensation dominates, and sometimes the two processes are in equilibrium—for every molecule evaporating, another is condensing. Which process takes the lead depends on the temperature of the air, the amount of water vapor in the air, and the accumulated liquid water on the Earth's surface.

In warmer temperatures, water molecules move more quickly and evaporation exceeds condensation. In cooler temperatures, water vapor molecules slow down enough to bond and become liquid, so condensation is more prevalent.

When condensation turns into precipitation, moisture replenishes the Earth. Calculations have been done which show that the amount of water that accumulates from precipitation, in the end, is equal to the amount that evaporates. It is crucial that this happens. Without this balance, the water cycle would eventually cease to exist.

Teaching about the Water Cycle

Understanding the water cycle is dependent on believing that both water and air are conserved, that matter is not lost during transitions from one phase of water to another, that air exists as a permanent, continuous substance. Studies* show this view is adopted by children around the ages of 9 or 10. Children continue to build on this basic notion, adding the idea of gravitation to explain rainfall (drops become heavy and fall) between the ages of 11 and 15. These findings, along with others in studies, remind us that we cannot assume children have a scientifically accurate grasp of the water cycle just because we have presented the facts through activities or text. It all depends on where they are in their conceptual development.

* Bar, Varda. "Children's Views about the Water Cycle." *Science Education 73(4)*. John Wiley and Sons, Inc. 1989.

The Water Cycle

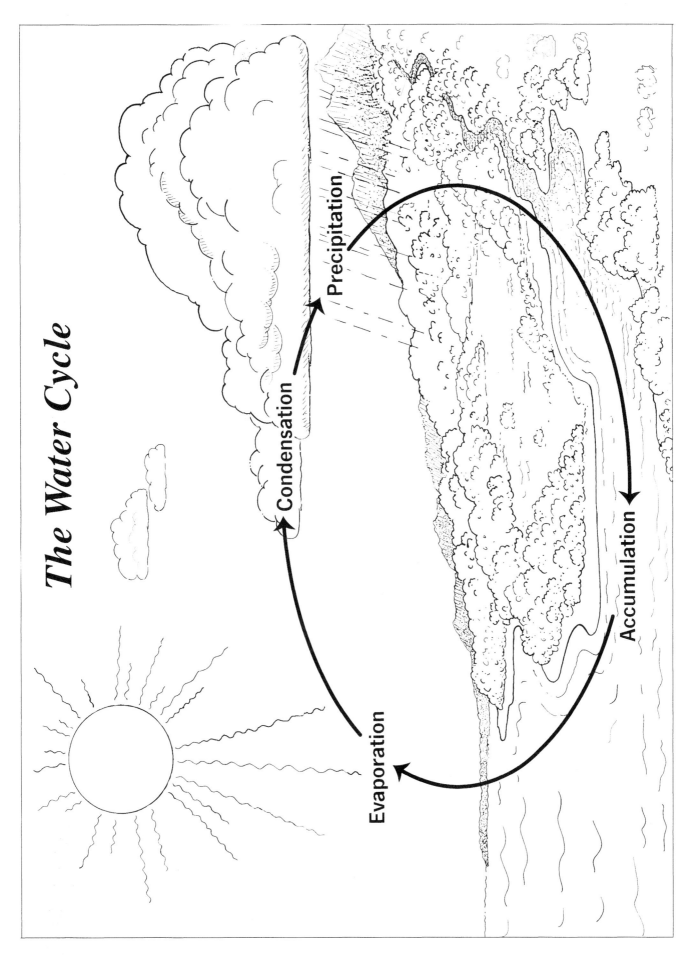

Moisture Proverbs

Proverbs are short, common-sense sayings based on people's observations. Which ones do you think are accurate predictors of weather? Design an investigation to test one of the proverbs.

Insects and Animals

If bees stay at home,
Rain will soon come.
If they fly away,
Fine will be the day.

When black snails on the road you see,
Then on the morrow rain will be.

If cats lick themselves, fair weather.

When sheep collect and huddle,
Tomorrow will become a puddle.

How long?

Sunshiny shower
Lasts half an hour.

The sharper the blast
The sooner 'tis past.

Rain long foretold, long last;
Short notice, soon past.

Sky

Red sky at night, sailor's delight.
Red sky in the morning, sailor's warning.

Rainbow in the morning
Shepherds take warning.
Rainbow toward night,
Shepherds delight.

Hair

When human hair becomes limp,
rain is near.

When combs crackle in your hair,
Look for weather clear and fair.

Moisture Proverbs

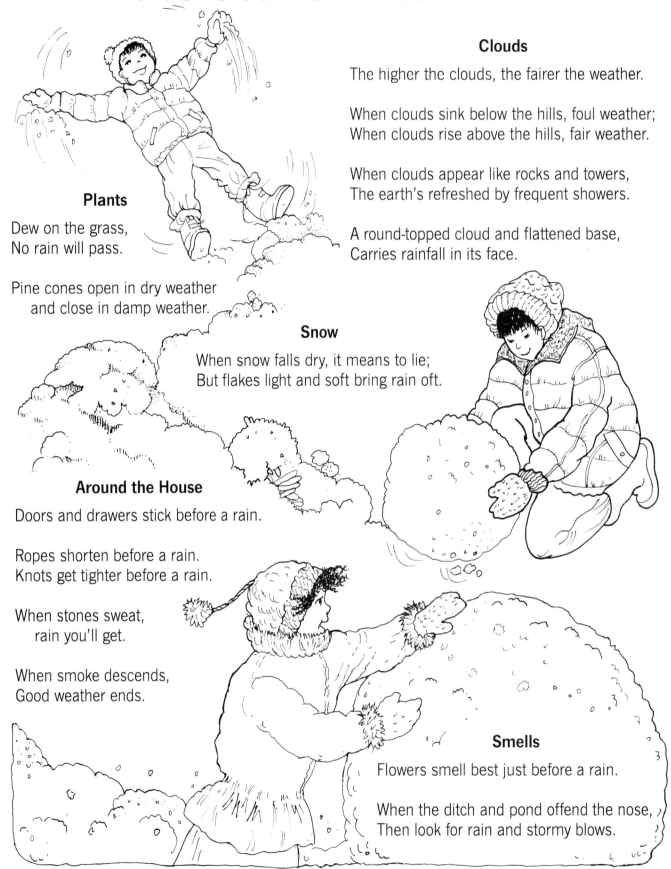

Clouds

The higher the clouds, the fairer the weather.

When clouds sink below the hills, foul weather;
When clouds rise above the hills, fair weather.

When clouds appear like rocks and towers,
The earth's refreshed by frequent showers.

A round-topped cloud and flattened base,
Carries rainfall in its face.

Plants

Dew on the grass,
No rain will pass.

Pine cones open in dry weather
and close in damp weather.

Snow

When snow falls dry, it means to lie;
But flakes light and soft bring rain oft.

Around the House

Doors and drawers stick before a rain.

Ropes shorten before a rain.
Knots get tighter before a rain.

When stones sweat,
  rain you'll get.

When smoke descends,
Good weather ends.

Smells

Flowers smell best just before a rain.

When the ditch and pond offend the nose,
Then look for rain and stormy blows.

Moisture Proverbs

Teacher Notes

"The trouble with weather proverbs is not so much that they're all wrong, but that they're not all right for all times in all places."

NOAA reprint of "Weather Proverbs" by R.E. Spencer (1979)

How long?	Comments
Sunshiny shower *Lasts half an hour.*	Sun shining through clouds indicates clouds breaking up at the end of a storm.
The sharper the blast *The sooner 'tis past.*	Cold-front storms, often the most violent, build rapidly and pass quickly.
Rain long foretold, long last; *Short notice, soon past.*	Warm-front storms, bringing mild rains, move slowly while the more violent cold-front storms move quickly.

Insects and Animals	
If bees stay at home, *Rain will soon come.* *If they fly away,* *Fine will be the day.*	Bees are good forecasters. As humidity rises, indicating stormy weather is coming, bees head for the hive where it is safe and dry.
When black snails on the road you see, *Then on the morrow rain will be.*	When away from moist environments, snails need humid air. High humidity is likely to lead to rain.
If cats lick themselves, * fair weather.*	During fair weather, with low relative humidity, static electricity can build up on cats. When a cat licks itself, the moisture makes its fur more conductive so the charge can "leak" off the cat.
When sheep collect and huddle, *Tomorrow will become a puddle.*	European sheepherders have observed this.

Sky	
Red sky at night, sailor's delight. *Red sky in the morning, sailor's warning.*	This refers to unusually red sunsets and is generally true although there are complicated and competing explanations. Gary Lockhart *(The Weather Companion)* cites a study that found about seven out of ten excessively red *sunsets* in northern climates were followed by good weather. Likewise, about seven out of ten very red *sunrises* were followed by rain within 24 hours.
Rainbow in the morning *Shepherds take warning.* *Rainbow toward night,* *Shepherds delight.*	In the U.S., storms usually move from west to east. A morning rainbow appears when the eastern sun shines on an approaching storm from the west. An evening rainbow is seen in the west when a storm has already passed.

Hair	
When human hair becomes limp, * rain is near.*	True. In fact, some hygrometers use a human hair to measure humidity.
When combs crackle in your hair, *Look for weather clear and fair.*	In low humidity, static electricity builds up in hair. Also see the proverb about cats.

Clouds

The higher the clouds, the fairer the weather.

When clouds sink below the hills,
*   foul weather;*
When clouds rise above the hills,
*   fair weather.*

When clouds appear like rocks and towers,
The earth's refreshed by frequent showers.

A round-topped cloud and flattened base,
Carries rainfall in its face.

Plants

Dew on the grass,
No rain will pass.

Pine cones open in dry weather
*   and close in damp weather.*

Snow

When snow falls dry, it means to lie;
But flakes light and soft bring rain oft.

Around the House

Doors and drawers stick before a rain.

Ropes shorten before a rain.
Knots get tighter before a rain.

When stones sweat,
*   rain you'll get.*

When smoke descends,
Good weather ends.

Smells

Flowers smell best just before a rain.

When the ditch and pond offend the nose,
Then look for rain and stormy blows.

Comments

Higher clouds indicate drier air and higher air pressure, both conditions of fair weather. If the cloud base is low, the air will be moist and rain more likely.

A mass of warm, rising air drawing in sufficient moisture causes cumulus clouds to develop sharp vertical towers, producing rain.

Dew forms when the air is relatively dry and the skies are clear, conditions of a high-pressure, fair-weather system. The surface on which it forms must be colder than the dew-point temperature.

Pine cones are among the most reliable natural weather indicators. In dry weather, the scales shrink and spread out stiffly. When the scales absorb the moisture in damp air, they expand and become more pliable; the cone returns to its normal shape.

Dry snowflakes form in extremely cold air with low moisture. Soft fluffy snowflakes form in moist air and at temperatures near freezing; a slight temperature increase will turn the snow to rain.

Sticky doors indicate high humidity, a likely condition for rain. The moisture swells the cellulose fibers in wood and everything fits more tightly.

When humidity climbs, moisture is absorbed in ropes. The moisture causes the rope fibers to expand, making them fatter and shorter.

It takes a great deal of heat to make the temperature of stones rise very much. If the air is moist, their temperature may remain below the dew point while the surrounding air is above the dew point. The moisture then condenses on the cooler rocks. In Finland, smooth stones are kept outside homes to help predict the weather.

In high humidity (when rain is likely), smoke particles collect moisture in the air, become heavier, and fall downward.

Odors held captive by high air pressure escape as the barometer drops. A falling barometer often indicates a storm is approaching.

46

Puddle Pushers

Topic
Evaporation

Key Question
After it rains, what happens to the water in a puddle?

Focus
Students will observe that water in a puddle disappears (evaporates) after a period of time.

Guiding Documents
Project 2061 Benchmarks
- *The sun warms the land, air, and water.*
- *When liquid water disappears, it turns into a gas (vapor) in the air and can reappear as a liquid when cooled, or as a solid if cooled below the freezing point of water.*
- *Numbers and shapes—and operations on them—help to describe and predict things about the world around us.*
- *Length can be thought of as unit lengths joined together, area as a collection of unit squares, and volume as a set of unit cubes.*
- *Areas of irregular shapes can be found by dividing them into squares and triangles.*

NRC Standard
- *Materials can exist in different states—solid, liquid, and gas. Some common materials, such as water, can be changed from one state to another by heating or cooling.*

NCTM Standards 2000*
- *Understand such attributes as length, area, weight, volume, and size of angle and select the appropriate type of unit for measuring each attribute*
- *Develop strategies for estimating the perimeters, areas, and volumes of irregular shapes*
- *Collect data using observations, surveys, and experiments*

Math
Measurement
    length
    area
    time
Estimation

Science
Physical science
    states of matter
Earth science
    meteorology
        water cycle

Integrated Processes
Observing
Predicting
Collecting and recording data
Comparing and contrasting
Interpreting data
Generalizing
Applying

Materials
String
White glue
Water
Small plastic cups
Chalk
Metric tapes
Centimeter grid paper

Background Information
We live on a water planet—70% is covered with oceans and seas, and of the rest, a high percentage is covered by lakes, ponds, rivers, streams, etc. Considering the entire planet, there is plenty of water on Earth; we will never run short. As a matter of fact, there is as much water on our planet today as there was 100 years ago, even 1000 years ago, 5000 years ago, etc. Because water moves through a cycle (evaporation, condensation, precipitation, accumulation), the amount of water remains constant.

The ocean is ultimately the source of most of the precipitation that falls on the land. Air masses moving over the water pick up large quantities that have *evaporated*. When these air masses move over the continents, much of this water falls out of the clouds (*condensation*) as *precipitation*. On land the water can infiltrate the ground, or evaporate into the air, or run off into rivers, lakes, and eventually the ocean (*accumulation*).

In this activity students will observe the disappearance of puddles (evaporation) after precipitation has occurred. They will determine the perimeter and surface area of the puddles at established time intervals.

Management
1. This activity needs to be done on concrete or asphalt so the water does not infiltrate the surface. Because the weather in some areas may not cooperate with your agenda, you may have to make your own puddles.

2. The area selected for puddle observations needs to be secured during the observation period so the puddles can remain undisturbed. You may want to post signs or rope off the area so that others will know not to tamper with the site.

3. To determine the time intervals between the observations, consider the existing conditions which will influence the evaporation rate (Is it cloudy or sunny? Is there a breeze? What is the temperature? ...the humidity?).

4. Students should work in groups of four or five.

5. White glue and water should be mixed prior to the activity. Use a ratio of 1:1. Pour about 50 mL of this mixture into one plastic cup per group. This mixture will be used to preserve the "perimeter" measures of each puddle ring.

6. Use string (not yarn) for making measurements. If colored string is available, use a different color for each puddle measure. The students could then color code their data.

7. Cut three or four lengths of string for each group. The lengths will depend on the sizes of the puddles. Students can trim the strings as they measure.

Procedure

1. After a rain (real or artificial), give each group a piece of chalk and take them outside to the concrete/asphalt surface that has been selected.

2. Have groups select a puddle and write their group's name beside it so they can use the same puddle for each observation.

3. Direct the students to use their chalk to draw around the perimeter of the puddle—make a "puddle ring"—and mark the time of day next to it.

4. Return to the classroom. Have students record the time of the observation on their activity sheet. Ask students to predict what will happen to their puddles after ___ minutes.

5. Wait the determined time interval and repeat this procedure at least three more times.

6. At the end of the observation period, tell students that they will now meaure their puddle rings.

7. Give each group as many strings as observations were made. Tell them that they will wrap the first string over the first chalk-drawn puddle ring. Direct them to cut the string to that length. Have them measure and record the length on their activity sheet. They should do this for all puddle rings.

8. Distribute plastic cups with the white glue and water. Instruct the students to immerse their strings, one at a time, in this mixture.

9. The soaked strings should be positioned around the puddle rings and be left to dry. (The drying process may take two hours or more depending upon weather conditions.) All puddle rings should be done this way.

10. When the strings are dry and stiff, have students gently lift them from the surface and take them back to the classroom.

11. Ask students to estimate the area covered by the puddle from the first measurement. Solicit ideas of how they could determine the area.

12. Let students explore various strategies, then if not already suggested, distribute the grid paper and inform students that they can count the square centimeters that fall within the stiffened strings.

13. Have students record their area measurements.

Discussion

1. What did you notice about the puddle rings during your observations? [They got smaller (unless it rained).] Why did this happen? [The water evaporated.]

2. What happened to the perimeters of the puddle rings during your observations? [They decreased.]

3. Did they decrease consistently? [not necessarily] How could you tell? [by looking at the data table]

4. How did you determine the areas of the puddles?

5. If you used the grid paper, were there any problems with this strategy? [what to do with squares that weren't completely within the puddle ring]

6. How could you solve these problems?

7. How did your puddle's size compare with another group's?

8. Did all the water in your puddle disappear? Was it the same for everyone? What could be some reasons for the differences?

9. What did you learn from this activity? [The water in the puddle evaporated. We were able to experience three of the four parts of the water cycle: precipitation, accumulation, and evaporation. The water changed from a liquid into a gas.]

 Journal Prompt: Tell the story of a rain puddle. Be sure to include how and where it forms and how it disappears.

Connections

The sun's heat energy warms the Earth, causing some water molecules to quicken and break free into the atmosphere as invisible water vapor. Heat energy puts the water cycle into motion. Observing and measuring a shrinking puddle provides evidence of evaporation. Would the same puddle evaporate in the same amount of time on another day? Does the rate of evaporation change? If so, what affects it? Those questions will be explored in the next activity, *Going, Going, Gone!*

Puddle Pushers

Puddle Ring	Perimeter	Surface Area

On a large piece of chart paper, write a story about your puddle using pictures, words, and numbers.

Puddle Pushers

Going, Going, Gone!

Topics
Evaporation
Scientific method

Key Questions
1. How can you make a wet handprint disappear?
2. How can the rate of evaporation be changed, if at all?

Focus
After experimenting with making a wet handprint on a paper towel disappear, students will use the scientific method to test variables which may affect the rate of evaporation and relate these variables to weather conditions.

Guiding Documents
Project 2061 Benchmarks
- *When liquid water disappears, it turns into a gas (vapor) in the air and can reappear as a liquid when cooled, or as a solid if cooled below the freezing point of water. Clouds and fog are made of tiny droplets of water.*
- *Scientists do not pay much attention to claims about how something they know about works unless the claims are backed up with evidence that can be confirmed and with a logical argument.*
- *Keep a notebook that describes observations made, carefully distinguishes actual observations from ideas and speculations about what was observed, and is understandable weeks or months later.*
- *Recognize when comparisons might not be fair because some conditions are not kept the same.*

NRC Standards
- *Plan and conduct a simple investigation.*
- *Employ simple equipment and tools to gather data and extend the senses.*
- *Materials can exist in different states—solid, liquid, and gas. Some common materials, such as water, can be changed from one state to another by heating or cooling.*
- *Water, which covers the majority of the earth's surface, circulates through the crust, oceans, and atmosphere in what is known as the "water cycle." Water evaporates from the earth's surface, rises and cools as it moves to higher elevations, condenses as rain or snow, and falls to the surface where it collects in lakes, oceans, soil, and in rocks underground.*

NCTM Standards 2000*
- *Select and apply appropriate standard units and tools to measure length, area, volume, weight, time, temperature, and the size of angles*
- *Collect data using observations, surveys, and experiments*
- *Represent data using tables and graphs such as line plots, bar graphs, and line graphs*
- *Propose and justify conclusions and predictions that are based on data and design studies to further investigate the conclusions or predictions*

Math
Measurement
    time
    volume (amount of water)
    distance, optional
    temperature, optional
Whole number operations
    subtraction (elasped time)
Graphing
    bar

Science
Earth science
    meteorology
        water cycle

Integrated Processes
Observing
Collecting and recording data
Comparing and contrasting
Identifying and controlling variables
Interpreting data
Relating

Materials
Paper towels, preferably brown
Water
Water containers for dipping hands
Tools for measuring water (see *Management 1*)
Clock or watch, preferably showing seconds
Other materials dependent on group plans
    (see *Management 2*)
12" x 18" construction paper or a file folder, one
    per group
Scissors
Glue

Background Information

The Water Cycle

Water can change from liquid to gas to solid, all states of matter which occur in the water cycle. Through evaporation, the liquid in a lake changes to water vapor and rises into the air. Depending on temperature and other weather conditions, the water vapor will eventually condense and fall again to Earth as liquid (rain) or solid (snow, sleet, or hail).

Evaporation Variables

The rate of evaporation varies due to 1) heat, 2) wind, 3) relative humidity, and 4) surface area. Water evaporates more quickly as the heat from the sun intensifies, the wind strengthens, the relative humidity decreases, and the surface area expands. Clothes dryers, hair dryers, light bulbs, and fans simulate nature by applying "heat" and/or "wind" to hurry the drying process.

The focus here is on heat and wind, and to a lesser extent, on surface area. Outdoors, comparisons can be made between sunny and shady spots or windy and wind-shielded locations. Indoors, heat can be generated by a light bulb and wind by a fan, for example. Relative humidity, preferably below 70%, is controlled by performing all the investigations at the same time. Students should control the kind of material and the amount of water used. When controlling indoor variables, also be aware of sunny versus shady areas of the room and blowing air from a furnace or air conditioner.

Children's Concepts about Evaporation

Since evaporation is an abstract concept, it is wise to ponder what we expect children to learn from doing evaporation activities. A fascinating research study was done with students, ranging in age from five to eleven years old, in the late 1980s in England[1].

"A great majority of children did not discuss water as a substance having varying states." When asked where the water had gone, younger children tended to mention clouds which are visible rather than air which is invisible. Because evaporation is difficult to see and occurs over a longer period of time, it is harder to grasp.

When asked, "Can the water be made to go faster or slower?," most thought it was *not possible*. When encouraged to test this, children more frequently tested slowing down evaporation, making water last longer, than speeding up evaporation.

Many had difficulty relating everyday experiences such as clothes drying to the formal water cycle model which usually depicts a large body of water as the source for evaporation. "There may be very little understanding of the process behind the cycle until children have reached the age of ten or eleven, and even then, only by a limited number of children." To broaden children's perspectives, a journal prompt and page for illustrating sources of evaporating water have been included in this activity.

Can children's understanding be changed? Yes. The researchers felt it was important for the children themselves to suggest the tests and the teacher to take the role of ensuring that the experiments were carried out in a fair way (controlling variables) rather than one of providing instruction. "This role required teachers to develop a questioning technique which would encourage children to pursue the implications of their ideas in action in a disciplined manner."

In this activity, we can expect students to discover that the rate of evaporation changes. However, we should not expect them to completely incorporate this understanding into the bigger picture of the water cycle. We are laying the groundwork for future learning and conceptual development.

1. Russell, Terry and Watt, Dorothy. *Primary SPACE Project Research Report: Evaporation and Condensation*. Liverpool University Press. PO Box 147, Liverpool, England L69 3BX. 1990.

Management

1. The small amount of water applied to the paper towels may be measured with an eyedropper, an oral syringe, a measuring spoon, or a graduated cylinder.
2. Additional materials will depend on what the groups (two to four students) want to try and teacher approval. For indoor tests, consider portable fans, light bulbs in sockets, hair dryers, or a piece of cardboard used as a fan. If the weather is cooperative, outdoor tests might include sun versus shade and a windy location versus one shielded from the wind.
3. More than one group can use the same method, but encourage variations such as different light bulb wattages, different fan speeds, or different distances from the paper.
4. If possible, do this activity when the relative humidity is less than 70%. Evaporation slows considerably as the air approaches saturation, making differences being tested less noticeable.
5. This activity may be spread over a week, as students progress from the introductory wet handprint to the design, implementation, and presentation of their findings.

Procedure

Part One

1. Present the opening scenario on the first activity page. Explain that the "paper on hand" is paper towels. Dip your hand in water and press it for a few seconds against a paper towel, pushing with the other hand to make it as flat as possible. Ask the first *Key Question,* "How can you make the wet handprint disappear?" Have students think about this silently while distributing the page, cut in half.

2. Instruct each student to get a paper towel, make a wet handprint, and try to dry it quickly without special equipment. Blowing and fanning are two options.
3. Have students record the time needed to dry the handprint and describe their methods. Help, as needed, in determining elapsed time using a clock face or by subtraction.
4. Guide class sharing of methods and drying times. Ask them for questions or concerns they have. Lead into a discussion of a fair test, the key to making valid comparisons. For example:

Mr. Morris: How did you try to dry your paper towel? How long did it take? (Have all the groups report.)
Mr. Morris: Which method seemed to work the best? (Have students identify the shortest drying time and method used.)
Shauna: I'm not so sure that was the best. What if we had just left the paper alone? Would it have dried just as fast?
Mr. Morris: That's a good question. We should set up an experiment to test that.
Sergio: Wait a minute. Some handprints had more water on them than others. No fair.
Mr. Morris: How could we make sure everyone uses the same amount of water?
Anna: Measure it.
Mr. Morris: How would you measure it?
Paul: An eyedropper might work.
Mr. Morris: Would you put the drops on your hand?
Chao: You could, but it might be easier to just squeeze them out on the paper.

Part Two
1. Continue the discussion, explaining that students will be doing further testing to answer the second *Key Question,* "How can the rate of evaporation be changed, if at all?"

Mr. Morris: What other things, besides the amount of water, need to be kept the same?
Esmeralda: We should all use the same kind of paper. One kind of paper might dry faster than another kind.
Tyrone: We should do the tests at the same time.
Mr. Morris: Why?
Tyrone: Because it is warmer in the afternoon than in the morning, and that might make a difference.
Mr. Morris: That's an interesting thought.
Kelly: I wonder if it makes a difference if we pile the water up in one spot on the paper towel or if we spread it around a bigger area?
Mr. Morris: Let's write down these ideas to help us with our planning. To do a scientific test, we need to make everything the same except the variable we are testing.

2. Divide the class into groups and give them the *Planning* page.
3. Have groups discuss possible ways to change the rate of evaporation and decide on the method they want to try. After obtaining your approval—based on safety, available materials, and variation from other group proposals—instruct the students to complete the page.

4. Give students time to collect the necessary supplies. Discuss whether timing will be done to the nearest minute or nearest second.
5. Have groups implement their plans and prepare a display of their investigation on large construction paper or a file folder (see illustrated samples).
6. Ask each group to use their display to make an oral presentation to the class. When all the groups have finished, hold a concluding discussion.

Discussion
1. Was your test fair? Explain how you controlled variables.
2. What different ways were used to try to change the rate of evaporation?
3. What did we learn about the rate of evaporation? [It can change.] Did the results surprise you?
4. What experiences have you had, besides this investigation, that make you think water sometimes evaporates more quickly or more slowly?
5. How do the ways we used to evaporate water relate to nature? [Fans are like the wind, light bulbs give off heat and light like the sun, and hair dryers are like the wind and sun combined.]
6. Under what conditions on Earth would a lot of water evaporate? [a hot day with strong winds]
7. If you were in a desert, how could you keep water from evaporating quickly? [protect from heat and wind by finding shade, keeping the water in a closed container so it can't escape into the air, insulating the container with crushed newspapers or another material, etc.]
8. What further testing would you like to try?
9. Challenge: What else, besides heat and wind, might affect the evaporation rate of water? [amount of relative humidity, amount of wet surface area (See *Extension 1.*)]

 Journal prompt: Make a list of local sources of evaporating water, both outdoors and indoors.

Follow journal writing with the *Evaporation* page. Have students draw a variety of settings where water evaporates. Encourage them to continue adding to their picture collection as they think of more. Though large bodies of water are most significant, students should realize that all of these sources contribute to the water cycle.

Outdoors	*Indoors*
ocean	wet paint
lake	wet hair
river	wet streak on chalkboard
puddle	aquarium
rain on a street	dog dish
wet footprints on a sidewalk	kitchen counter wiped
wet clothes on a line	with wet cloth
dew on grass	filled bathtub
sweaty person	running shower
car washing	
dripping faucet	
swimming pool	

Extensions

1. To compare how surface area might affect the evaporation rate, do the activity *Rain Away* (AIMS®, February 1991 – Volume V, Number 7). Relate this to the importance of oceans, with their large surface area, in the water cycle.
2. Hold an evaporation race. Have student groups use one or a combination of methods to make 50 mL of water in a container evaporate most quickly.

* Reprinted with permission from *Principles and Standards for School Mathematics,* 2000 by the National Council of Teachers of Mathematics. All rights reserved.

Connections

The unequal heating of the Earth causes differences in evaporation rates. The warmer it is, the faster water molecules move and evaporate into the air and the greater the air's capacity for moisture. Air masses with contrasting temperatures and pressures put the air in motion, another factor in increasing the rate of evaporation.

All this evaporation adds moisture to the air and increases humidity. In *Sling Fling*, a simple tool will be constructed to measure the relative humidity.

Going, Going, Gone!

You wrapped a birthday present for a friend using paper on hand and a colorful bow. Just as you were leaving for the party, your wet hand left a print on the gift.

How can you make the wet handprint disappear?

Starting Time	Finishing Time	Elasped Time

Describe what you did.

Going, Going, Gone!

You wrapped a birthday present for a friend using paper on hand and a colorful bow. Just as you were leaving for the party, your wet hand left a print on the gift.

How can you make the wet handprint disappear?

Starting Time	Finishing Time	Elasped Time

Describe what you did.

Going, Going, Gone!

How can the rate of evaporation be changed, if at all?

Materials
2 paper towels

Prediction

Procedure
Wet two paper towels. Leave one alone and dry the other in a different way.
(Or if outdoors, put in two different locations.)

How are the two environments/tests alike? (variables controlled)

How are they different? (variable tested)

Collecting Data
Record your measurements and make a graph on another page.

Conclusion

Going, Going, Gone!

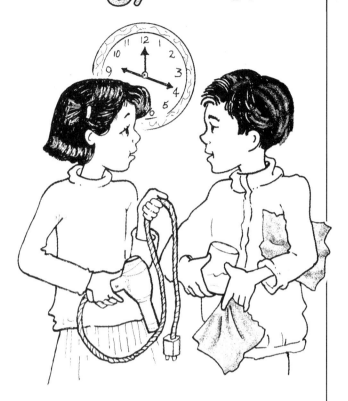

Make a poster on 12" x 18" construction paper.

How can the rate of evaporation be changed, if at all?

Prediction

We think the 2 towels will take the same amount of time to dry.

Materials

2 paper towels
water
5 mL measuring spoon
watch on clock

Procedure

1. Each towel gets 5 mL of water sprinkled a little here and a little there.
2. One paper is put in the sun and the other in the shade. Other weather conditions, like humidity and wind are the same.
3. Time how long each towel takes to evaporate.

Time Table

Time	Sun	Shade
Start	11:24	11:24
Finish	11:30	11:35
Elapsed	6 min.	11 min.

Towel Evaporation

(Bar graph: Elapsed Time (minutes) 0–12; Sun = 6, Shade = 11)

Conclusion

The sun made the water evaporate faster.

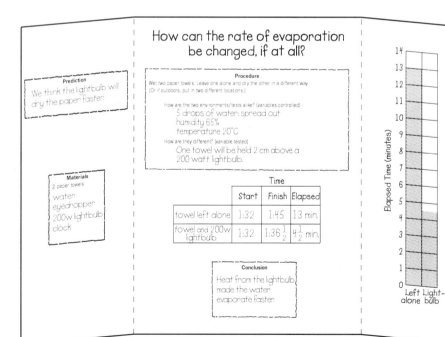

How can the rate of evaporation be changed, if at all?

Prediction

We think the lightbulb will dry the paper faster.

Procedure

Wet two paper towels. Leave one alone and dry the other in a different way. (Or if outdoors, put in two different locations.)

How are the two environments/tests alike? (variables controlled)
5 drops of water; spread out
humidity 65%
temperature 20°C

How are they different? (variable tested)
One towel will be held 2 cm above a 200 watt lightbulb.

Materials

2 paper towels
water
eyedropper
200w lightbulb
clock

Time

	Start	Finish	Elapsed
towel left alone	1:32	1:45	13 min.
towel and 200w lightbulb	1:32	$1:36\frac{1}{2}$	$4\frac{1}{2}$ min.

Conclusion

Heat from the lightbulb made the water evaporate faster.

(Bar graph: Elapsed Time (minutes) 0–14; Left-alone = 13, Light-bulb = 4½)

Make a display board from a file folder or a large piece of construction paper.

Going, Going, Gone!

Evaporation

Draw several pictures showing from where water can evaporate.
They all contribute to the water cycle.

Topic
Weather station: relative humidity

Key Question
How can we measure the moisture in the air?

Focus
Students will construct a sling psychrometer with wet- and dry-bulb thermometers and use it, along with a table, to find the relative humidity.

Guiding Documents
Project 2061 Benchmarks
- *Measuring instruments can be used to gather accurate information for making scientific comparisons of objects and events and for designing and constructing things that will work properly.*
- *When liquid water disappears, it turns into a gas (vapor) in the air and can reappear as a liquid when cooled, or as a solid if cooled below the freezing point of water. Clouds and fog are made of tiny droplets of water.*

NRC Standards
- *Weather changes from day to day and over the seasons. Weather can be described by measurable quantities, such as temperature, wind direction and speed, and precipitation.*
- *Tools help scientists make better observations, measurements, and equipment for investigations. They help scientists see, measure, and do things that they could not otherwise see, measure, and do.*
- *Water, which covers the majority of the earth's surface, circulates through the crust, oceans, and atmosphere in what is known as the "water cycle." Water evaporates from the earth's surface, rises and cools as it moves to higher elevations, condenses as rain or snow, and falls to the surface where it collects in lakes, oceans, soil, and in rocks underground.*

NCTM Standards 2000*
- *Select and apply appropriate standard units and tools to measure length, area, volume, weight, time, temperature, and the size of angles*
- *Collect data using observations, surveys, and experiments*
- *Represent data using tables and graphs such as line plots, bar graphs, and line graphs*

Math
Measurement
    temperature
Whole number operations
    subtraction
Graphs
    bar

Science
Earth science
    meteorology
        water cycle

Integrated Processes
Observing
Collecting and recording data
Comparing and contrasting
Interpreting data
Relating

Materials
For each group:
    2 thermometers with matching readings
        (see *Management 1*)
    corrugated cardboard slightly larger than
        thermometers
    strip of gauze or about 4 cm of white cotton shoelace
    string or twine, about 60 cm
    scissors
    hole punch (see *Management 2*)
    transparent tape
    water

Background Information
Relative humidity
    Humidity is the amount of water vapor in the air. One factor affecting humidity is the amount of available water. There is great potential for evaporation over the oceans but little over the deserts where water is scarce. Humidity is also affected by the heat energy from the sun. The rate of evaporation increases in warmer temperatures and decreases in cooler temperatures.
    Relative humidity is the amount of water vapor in the air compared to the amount of water vapor that can be absorbed by the air at a given temperature. When no more water vapor can be absorbed, the air is saturated; it has 100% relative humidity. Relative humidity is the percentage of saturation. Warm air can absorb more water vapor than cold air.

High relative humidity does not necessarily mean high temperatures. In fact, high relative humidity is more likely to occur in cool temperatures because it takes less water vapor to saturate cold air. Daily relative humidity patterns are often the reverse of temperature patterns. In late afternoon, when the temperatures are usually highest, the relative humidity is generally the lowest. In the early morning, when temperatures are usually at their lowest, the relative humidity is likely at its highest.

Hygrometers

The amount of moisture in the air is measured by a hygrometer. Sometimes a hair hygrometer is used because human hair stretches when it is humid. Another kind of hygrometer is a psychrometer, based on the principle that evaporation causes cooling.

The sling psychrometer has two thermometers. One is kept dry and the other has cotton material, which has been wet, covering the bulb. Scientists use clean muslin cloth and distilled water. Commercial sling psychrometers have a handle which is used to whirl the psychrometer through the air at about four revolutions per second.

As the psychrometer is whirled, water evaporates from the cloth and cools the thermometer. The wet-bulb temperature reflects the lowest temperature to which the air, at that moment, can be cooled by evaporation. The lower the humidity, the more quickly water can evaporate into the air and the cooler the wet-bulb temperature. So the lower the humidity, the greater the temperature differences between the wet- and dry-bulb thermometers. If the relative humidity is 100%, there will be no difference between the temperatures of the two thermometers.

Children's concepts about relative humidity

Since water vapor in the air is invisible, relative humidity is difficult to understand. Children will probably most readily relate to how damp (sticky) or dry the air makes them feel.

At least two naive conceptions that students may have about relative humidity have been identified. 1) *Low temperatures produce low relative humidity; high temperatures produce high relative humidity.* At lower temperatures, it takes less moisture to make the relative humidity high. As temperatures climb, more moisture must evaporate into the air for there to be high relative humidity. Low or high humidity can occur no matter what the air temperature is. 2) *The cooler temperature registered on a wet-bulb thermometer is due to cool water.* Just as we are cooled by sweat evaporating from our skin, the wet-bulb thermometer is cooled by water molecules evaporating from the wet cotton. The lower the humidity, the more molecules can evaporate and the cooler the wet-bulb temperature.

Management

1. For valid data, each pair of thermometers should have matching readings. However, variations from one pair to the next are acceptable.
2. To make holes in the cardboard, a hole punch is preferable for both safety and neatness.
3. To moisten the wet-bulb thermometer, dip the bulb and shoelace into water.
4. Outdoor measurements should be taken in a shaded, open area. Caution students to stand clear of obstacles and each other before whirling the psychrometer.
5. A relative humidity table with one-degree increments is appropriate for temperatures read to the nearest degree. Though the percentage jumps are sometimes large, students can be challenged to read "between the lines" (see *Discussion 4*).
6. For temperature readings that extend beyond the table, search for a calculator on the Internet.

Procedure

1. Ask, "How do we know water evaporates?" [A puddle of water disappeared. The wet clothes on the line dried.] "When you are playing outdoors, do you sometimes feel sticky?" Tell students that happens when there is a lot of water vapor (moisture) in the air, the part of weather they will be measuring today.
2. Distribute the *Construction* page to each group. Explain that they will be making a sling psychrometer, one of the tools used by meteorologists to measure the air's moisture. Review the directions and have groups gather the materials and construct the psychrometer.
3. Outside, in a shaded, open area, wait for the thermometers to stabilize and then demonstrate how to use the sling psychrometer. Ask for predictions: "Do you think the thermometers will have the same readings? If not, which thermometer do you think will have a higher temperature reading?"
4. Instruct groups to whirl their psychrometers about one minute, then check the wet-bulb temperature. Have them resume whirling and checking until the wet-bulb temperature is no longer falling, then read both thermometers.
5. Return indoors and distribute the recording page. Ask, "Which thermometer had a higher temperature reading?" [dry-bulb thermometer, unless the relative humidity is 100% in which case the temperatures are the same] "Why do you think the wet-bulb temperature is lower?" [the water evaporating from the wet shoelace causes cooling]

6. Direct students to find the difference between the dry- and wet-bulb temperatures, then use the printed table to find the relative humidity. To better focus on the needed data, suggest students lightly color the *dry-bulb temperature* row and the *difference* row in their handwritten tables.

7. Have students graph their data and make statements based on the graph.

8. Continue having students collect relative humidity data at a certain time(s) each day as part of an on-going weather station. Relative humidity does not have a designated location on the station model, however.

Discussion

1. How do our results compare with official reports from the National Weather Service or other media? (Hourly reports are available on many weather websites.)

2. Will the humidity be higher when there is a small or a large difference in the temperature readings of the two thermometers. [small difference] Explain. [A small difference means high humidity because very little water from the wet-bulb thermometer could evaporate into the air and cool it down.]

3. If the wet- and dry-bulb temperatures are the same, what would be the relative humidity? [100%]

4. What is your estimate of the relative humidity if the dry-bulb temperature is 22°C and the difference between wet- and dry-bulb temperatures is about 2.5°C? [79 or 80%] Explain your thinking. [Those percentages are halfway between the 83% in the "2" column and the 76% in the "3" column.]

5. How is a sling psychrometer like sweating skin? [Evaporation from the wet shoelace causes cooling just like evaporating sweat cools the skin.]

6. Why would a desert have low relative humidity? [There is a general lack of water to evaporate, and warm air, typical in many deserts, needs more water vapor than cold air to increase the relative humidity.]

7. In winter, why might our skin feel dry and rough? (Warm indoor temperatures combined with low humidity cause the moisture on our skin to evaporate quickly.)

Extension

What is the pattern of relative humidity over a day? Instruct students to track the relative humidity from hour to hour during one day, using both their sling psychrometers and website data. When is it greatest? [often in the early morning] When is it driest? [usually in late afternoon, after the sun has warmed the air]

Connections

Solar energy, which heats the Earth unequally, combined with the amount of available water largely determine how humid the air will be. The rate of evaporation increases as the temperature warms. But because warm air can absorb more water vapor, it requires more water vapor to reach saturation or 100% relative humidity than cold air. Without a sufficient water supply, however, evaporation will be limited at any temperature.

After learning how to measure relative humidity, we might wonder how it affects people's comfort. That is the topic of the next activity, *Apparently Hot.*

SLING FLING

Materials

2 thermometers with matching readings
Cardboard, about 4 cm x 20 cm
Strip of gauze or about 4 cm of white cotton shoelace
String or twine, about 60 cm
Scissors
Hole punch, optional
Transparent tape
Water

Constructing the sling psychrometer

1. Tie a strip of gauze or slide the piece of shoelace over the bulb of one thermometer. Place this thermometer so that the bulb is below the edge of the cardboard. Mark the thermometer hole at the top, then make a small hole at that mark with a hole punch.

2. Center the other thermometer on the other side of the cardboard. Mark and make another hole for it.

3. Securely attach the thermometers with string at the upper end and transparent tape at the lower end. Devise a way to pass one string through both holes or use one string each. Leave an extra 15 to 20 cm of string for gripping, making a large knot or a small loop at the end.

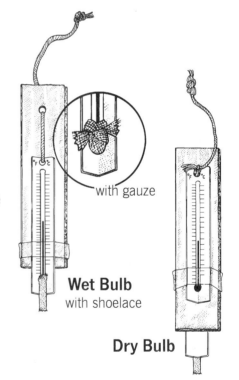

with gauze

Wet Bulb
with shoelace

Dry Bulb

Using the psychrometer

Dip the bottom of the gauze or shoelace in water. Watch the water travel until the part covering the thermometer bulb is completely wet. Take the psychrometer to an open area, away from buildings. Holding it by the end knot, swing it around in a circle for about one minute. When the temperature stops dropping, record the dry-bulb temperature and the wet-bulb temperature.

Find the difference between the dry-bulb and wet-bulb temperatures. Then use the table on another page to find the relative humidity.

Relative Humidity Table

Difference between wet- and dry-bulb temperatures (C°)

Dry-bulb temperature (C°)	1	2	3	4	5	6	7	8	9	10	11	12	13	14	15	16
0	81	64	46	29	13											
1	83	66	49	33	17											
2	84	68	52	37	22	7										
3	84	70	55	40	26	12										
4	85	71	57	43	29	16										
5	86	72	58	45	33	20	7									
6	86	73	60	48	35	24	11									
7	87	74	62	50	38	26	15									
8	87	75	63	51	40	29	19	8								
9	88	76	64	53	42	32	22	12								
10	88	77	66	55	44	34	24	15	6							
11	89	78	67	56	46	36	27	18	9							
12	89	78	68	58	48	39	29	21	12							
13	89	79	69	59	50	41	32	23	15	7						
14	90	79	70	60	51	42	34	26	18	10						
15	90	80	71	61	53	44	36	27	20	13	6					
16	90	81	71	63	54	46	38	30	23	15	8					
17	90	81	72	64	55	47	40	32	25	18	11					
18	91	82	73	65	57	49	41	34	27	20	14	7				
19	91	82	74	65	58	50	43	36	29	22	16	10				
20	91	83	74	66	59	51	44	37	31	24	18	12	6			
21	91	83	75	67	60	53	46	39	32	26	20	14	9			
22	92	83	76	68	61	54	47	40	34	28	22	17	11	6		
23	92	84	76	69	62	55	48	42	36	30	24	19	13	8		
24	92	84	77	69	62	56	49	43	37	31	26	20	15	10	5	
25	92	84	77	70	63	57	50	44	39	33	28	22	17	12	8	
26	92	85	78	71	64	58	51	46	40	34	29	24	19	14	10	5
27	92	85	78	71	65	58	52	47	41	36	31	26	21	16	12	7
28	93	85	78	72	65	59	53	48	42	37	32	27	22	18	13	9
29	93	86	79	72	66	60	54	49	43	38	33	28	24	19	15	11
30	93	86	79	73	67	61	55	50	44	39	35	30	25	21	17	13
31	93	86	80	73	67	61	56	51	45	40	36	31	27	22	18	14
32	93	86	80	74	68	62	57	51	46	41	37	32	28	24	20	16
33	93	87	80	74	68	63	57	52	47	42	38	33	29	25	21	17
34	93	87	81	75	69	63	58	53	48	43	39	35	30	26	23	19
35	94	87	81	75	69	64	59	54	49	44	40	36	32	28	24	20
36	94	87	81	75	70	64	59	54	50	45	41	37	33	29	25	21
37	94	87	82	76	70	65	60	55	51	46	42	38	34	30	26	23
38	94	88	82	76	71	66	61	56	51	47	43	39	35	31	27	24
39	94	88	82	77	71	66	61	57	52	48	43	39	36	32	28	25
40	94	88	82	77	72	67	62	57	53	48	44	40	36	33	29	26

Source: Bulletin of the U.S. Weather Bureau No. 1071

SLING FLING

SLING FLING

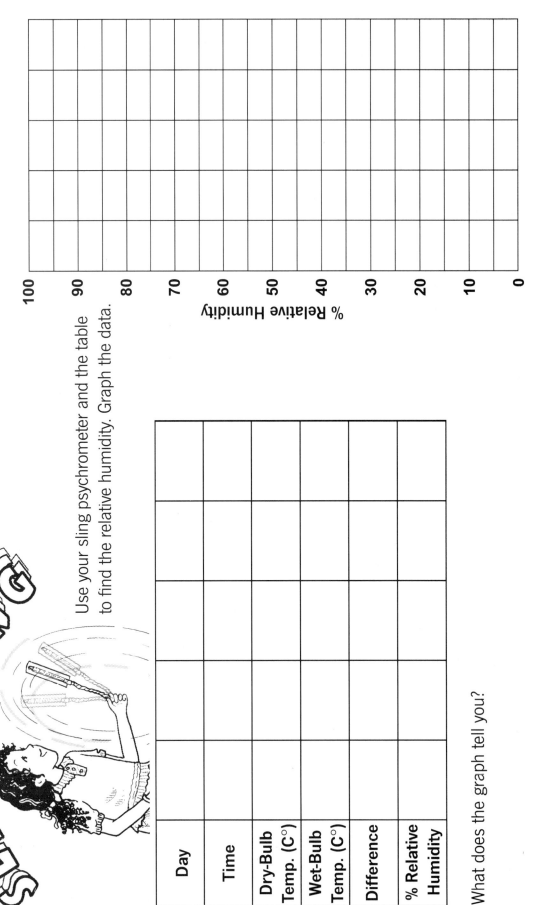

Use your sling psychrometer and the table to find the relative humidity. Graph the data.

Day					
Time					
Dry-Bulb Temp. (C°)					
Wet-Bulb Temp. (C°)					
Difference					
% Relative Humidity					

% Relative Humidity

100 90 80 70 60 50 40 30 20 10 0

Day/Time

What does the graph tell you?

Apparently HOT

Topic
Apparent or "feels-like" temperature
(temperature plus relative humidity)

Key Question
How does the moisture in the air affect how we feel?

Focus
Apparent temperature is to hot what *wind chill* is to cold. Students will use temperature and relative humidity data they have gathered, along with a table, to determine the apparent temperature. They will become aware of the effects of high apparent temperatures on people and recommended safety precautions.

Guiding Documents
Project 2061 Benchmarks
- *When liquid water disappears, it turns into a gas (vapor) in the air and can reappear as a liquid when cooled, or as a solid if cooled below the freezing point of water.*
- *Tables and graphs can show how values of one quantity are related to values of another.*

NRC Standards
- *Weather changes from day to day and over the seasons. Weather can be described by measurable quantities, such as temperature, wind direction and speed, and precipitation.*
- *Safety and security are basic needs of humans. Safety involves freedom from danger, risk, or injury. Security involves feelings of confidence and lack of anxiety and fear. Student understandings include following safety rules for home and school, preventing abuse and neglect, avoiding injury, knowing whom to ask for help, and when and how to say no.*

NCTM Standards 2000*
- *Select and apply appropriate standard units and tools to measure length, area, volume, weight, time, temperature, and the size of angles*
- *Collect data using observations, surveys, and experiments*

Math
Measurement
    temperature
Data analysis

Science
Earth science
    meteorology
        water cycle

Integrated Processes
Observing
Collecting and recording data
Comparing and contrasting
Interpreting data
Relating

Materials
Thermometer
Sling psychrometer (see *Sling Fling*)
Colored pencils

Background Information
The amount of moisture combined with air temperature affects how we feel. During hot temperatures, sweat evaporating from the body cools the skin. When the relative humidity is low, this moisture evaporates quickly, particularly if conditions are windy. We feel cool, though our skin may tend to become dry. But as the relative humidity climbs to 70% and above, the sweat cannot evaporate very effectively because there is little room for more water vapor in the air. We feel sticky and uncomfortable.

This feeling of discomfort can affect how we work. Military studies of radar operators working in tropical climates found that the operators made many more mistakes as the temperature and humidity rose. Their work also slowed down and they could work well for only short periods of time.

Law enforcement people have found riots are much more likely at temperatures between 29°C and 32°C (84°F and 90°F), especially if the humidity rises.

But high temperature and high relative humidity can also result in a variety of heat disorders and their severity tends to increase with age. "Heat cramps in a 17-year-old may be heat exhaustion in someone 40, and heat stroke in a person over 60." Those most at risk include elderly persons, small children, and the chronically ill.

Heat Disorders*

Heat Disorder	Symptoms	First Aid
Sunburn	Redness and pain. In severe cases swelling of skin, blisters, fever, headaches.	Ointments for mild cases if blisters appear and do not break. If breaking occurs, apply dry sterile dressing. Serious, extensive cases should be seen by physician.
Heat Cramps	Painful spasms usually in muscles of legs and abdomen possible. Heavy sweating.	Firm pressure on cramping muscles, or gentle massage to relieve spasm. Give sips of water. If nausea occurs, discontinue use.
Heat Exhaustion	Heavy sweating, weakness, skin cold, pale and clammy. Pulse weak. Normal temperature possible. Fainting and vomiting.	Get victim out of sun. Lay down and loosen clothing. Apply cool, wet cloths. Fan or move victim to air-conditioned room. Sips of water. If nausea occurs, discontinue use. If vomiting continues, seek immediate medical attention.
Heatstroke (or sunstroke)	High body temperature (106°F or higher). Hot dry skin. Rapid and strong pulse. Possible unconsciousness.	**Heatstroke is a severe medical emergency. Summon emergency medical assistance or get the victim to a hospital immediately. Delay can be fatal.** Move the victim to a cooler environment. Reduce body temperature with cold bath or sponging. Use extreme caution. Do not give fluids.

* National Oceanic and Atmospheric Administration (NOAA), National Weather Service/Federal Emergency Management Agency/American Red Cross. *Heat Wave* (brochure). NOAA/PA85001.

The Heat Index was developed by the National Weather Service in response to the number of deaths caused by the combination of high heat and high relative humidity. It gives "feels-like" or *apparent temperatures* and warns when weather conditions may be harmful. This is important because North American summers are hot and areas east of the Rockies, in particular, experience high relative humidity.

When the apparent temperature is expected to exceed 41°C (105°F), the National Weather Service issues alerts. Safety precautions include slowing down physical activities, dressing for summer, drinking plenty of water or other non-alcoholic fluids, spending more time in cool, air-conditioned places, and staying out of the sun as much as possible.

Management

1. Since apparent temperatures apply to hot weather, it is best to do this activity during the late spring, summer, or early fall.
2. It is assumed students are already acquainted with gathering temperature (*Temperature Tally* in *Weather Sense: Temperature, Air Pressure, and Wind*) and relative humidity (*Sling Fling*) data.
3. Both Celsius and Fahrenheit *Heat Indexes* are provided; use the one that corresponds to the measurements students will take. The Celsius table is a conversion of the Fahrenheit table developed by the National Weather Service. As such, some rounding occurred and temperature intervals vary.

Procedure

1. Ask, "Outdoors, do you ever feel warmer than the thermometer shows?" Among reasons given might be one that mentions "sticky" air being uncomfortable. Explain that a lot of moisture in the air can make the temperature feel hotter. Sometimes the combination of high temperatures and high relative humidity can be dangerous to the health of people who are at risk—the elderly, small children, those who are ill, etc.
2. Introduce the *Heat Index*. Use *Discussion* questions 1 through 3 to help students become acquainted with it.
3. Have students make a stair-step line dividing the *Heat Index* into two parts, temperatures at or above 41°C (105°F) and those below. Direct them to lightly color the temperatures in the upper part, the danger zone.

Air Temperature (C°)	0	5	10	15	20	25	30	35	40	45	50	55	60	65	70	75	80	85	90	95	100
60	52																				
57	49	53																			
54	47	50	55																		
52	44	47	51	55	61																
49	42	44	47	51	54	59	64														
46	39	42	44	46	49	53	57	62	66												
43	37	39	41	42	44	47	51	54	58	62	66										
41	35	36	38	39	41	43	45	48	51	54	57	61	65								
38	33	34	35	36	37	38	40	42	43	46	49	52	56	59	62						
35	31	31	32	33	34	34	36	37	38	40	42	43	46	48	51	54	58				
32	28	29	29	30	31	31	32	33	34	35	36	37	38	39	41	43	45	47	50		
29	26	26	27	27	28	28	29	29	30	31	31	32	32	33	34	35	36	37	39	41	42
27	23	23	24	24	25	25	26	26	26	27	27	27	28	28	29	30	30	31	31	32	33
24	21	21	21	22	22	22	23	23	23	23	24	24	24	24	25	25	26	26	26	26	27
21	18	18	18	18	19	19	19	19	20	20	21	21	21	21	21	21	22	22	22	22	22

4. Instruct students to use a thermometer and sling psychrometer (with its accompanying table) to measure the temperature and relative humidity, then use the *Heat Index* to determine the apparent or "feels like" temperature.

5. Discuss the effects of dangerous apparent temperatures—heat exhaustion, heat cramps, and heatstroke—and the safety precautions that can be taken. Precautions include staying out of the sun, reducing physical activity, and drinking plenty of water. Contribute additional advice from *Background Information* as appropriate.

Discussion

Getting acquainted with the Heat Index

1. What information do we need in order to use the *Heat Index*? [air temperature and relative humidity] What tools do we use to measure these? [thermometer and a sling psychrometer]

2. Look at the temperatures in the table. Can the relative humidity ever make us feel cooler than the thermometer says? [Yes, when the relative humidity is very low, particularly below 10%.]

3. When does the apparent temperature equal the air temperature? [Although this might be expected to be at 0% relative humidity, it varies from about 10% (at extremely high temperatures) on up. The lower the temperature, the higher the percent where the two temperatures match.]

Other questions

4. How does the moisture in the air affect how we feel? [The higher the relative humidity, the more slowly sweat evaporates into the air. It makes us feel warmer and more sticky. Low relative humidity can actually make the air seem cooler than it really is because faster evaporation cools us.]

5. Do you think high temperature and high relative humidity affect your work at school? How has your school tried to reduce the effects of temperature and humidity in your classroom? [The tightly-sealed rooms may keep humidity lower than outdoors. Air-conditioners, in addition to circulating cooler air, also tend to have a drying effect.]

6. How safe is the apparent temperature today? If it is in a warning zone, what are we advised to do? [stay in air-conditioned places or out of the sun, reduce physical activity, drink plenty of water]

Extensions

1. On the Internet, find a heat calculator for temperatures or a relative humidity not included on the activity page charts.

2. If your weather is not hot or humid enough, gather data for another location by contacting a school in a different part of the country or by consulting a weather website.

Curriculum Correlation

Art

Have students make posters illustrating safety precautions when days are dangerously hot and humid.

Multi-cultural

Relate how some cultures believe heat and humidity, under special circumstances, can benefit their health, e.g., Native American sweat houses, Swedish saunas, etc.

* Reprinted with permission from *Principles and Standards for School Mathematics,* 2000 by the National Council of Teachers of Mathematics. All rights reserved.

Connections

The cycling of water between Earth and the atmosphere is driven by the sun's heat energy. This energy causes water to evaporate, increasing the moisture in the air. People feel uncomfortable when the relative humidity is high because sweat, humans' cooling mechanism, does not easily evaporate into the saturated air. High temperatures combined with high relative humidity can have a dangerous effect on people. All of the above are part of the evaporation portion of the water cycle.

Evaporation can lead to condensation, the focus of the next series of activities.

Apparently HOT

Heat Index (Celsius)*

This chart was developed by the National Weather Service to warn people when being in the sun and/or physically active is dangerous. The "feels like" temperatures were developed for shady, light wind conditions. In full sunshine, temperatures can increase up to 8°C.

Relative Humidity (%)

Air Temp (C°)	0	5	10	15	20	25	30	35	40	45	50	55	60	65	70	75	80	85	90	95	100
60	52																				
57	49	53																			
54	47	50	55																		
52	44	47	51	55	61																
49	42	44	47	51	54	59	64														
46	39	42	44	46	49	53	57	62	66												
43	37	39	41	42	44	47	51	54	58	62	66										
41	35	36	38	39	41	43	45	48	51	54	57	61	65								
38	33	34	35	36	37	38	40	42	43	46	49	52	56	59	62						
35	31	31	32	33	34	34	36	37	38	40	42	43	46	48	51	54	58				
32	28	29	29	30	31	31	32	33	34	35	36	37	38	39	41	43	45	47	50		
29	26	26	27	27	28	28	29	29	30	31	31	32	32	33	34	35	36	37	39	41	42
27	23	23	24	24	25	25	26	26	26	27	27	27	28	28	29	30	30	31	31	32	33
24	21	21	21	22	22	22	23	23	23	23	24	24	24	24	25	25	26	26	26	26	27
21	18	18	18	18	19	19	19	19	20	20	21	21	21	21	21	21	22	22	22	22	22

Air Temperature (C°)

Color the feels-like temperatures of 41°C or higher. These temperatures can be dangerous.

Heat Index	Possible heat disorders of people in higher risk groups
54° or higher	Heatstroke or sunstroke highly likely with continued exposure.
41° – 54°	Sunstroke, heat cramps, or heat exhaustion likely, and heatstroke possible with prolonged exposure and/or physical activity.
32° – 41°	Sunstroke, heat cramps and heat exhaustion possible with prolonged exposure and/or physical activity.
27° – 32°	Fatigue possible with prolonged exposure and/or physical activity.

*Source: National Oceanic and Atmospheric Administration, National Weather Service/Federal Emergency Management Agency/American Red Cross. *Heat Wave* (brochure). NOAA/PA 85001. (converted from °F)

Heat Index (Fahrenheit)*

This chart was developed by the National Weather Service to warn people when being in the sun and/or physically active is dangerous. The "feels like" temperatures were developed for shady, light wind conditions. In full sunshine, temperatures can increase up to 15°F.

Relative Humidity (%)

Air Temperature (F°)	0	5	10	15	20	25	30	35	40	45	50	55	60	65	70	75	80	85	90	95	100
140	125																				
135	120	128																			
130	117	122	131																		
125	111	116	123	131	141																
120	107	111	116	123	130	139	148														
115	103	107	111	115	120	127	135	143	151												
110	99	102	105	108	112	117	123	130	137	143	150										
105	95	97	100	102	105	109	113	118	123	129	135	142	149								
100	91	93	95	97	99	101	104	107	110	115	120	126	132	138	144						
95	87	88	90	91	93	94	96	98	101	104	107	110	114	119	124	130	136				
90	83	84	85	86	87	88	90	91	93	95	96	98	100	102	106	109	113	117	122		
85	78	79	80	81	82	83	84	85	86	87	88	89	90	91	93	95	97	99	102	105	108
80	73	74	75	76	77	77	78	79	79	80	81	81	82	83	85	86	86	87	88	89	91
75	69	69	70	71	72	72	73	73	74	74	75	75	76	76	77	77	78	78	79	79	80
70	64	64	65	65	66	66	67	67	68	68	69	69	70	70	70	70	71	71	71	71	72

Color the feels-like temperatures of 105°F or higher. These temperatures can be dangerous.

Heat Index	Possible heat disorders of people in higher risk groups
130° or higher	Heatstroke or sunstroke highly likely with continued exposure.
105° – 130°	Sunstroke, heat cramps, or heat exhaustion likely, and heatstroke possible with prolonged exposure and/or physical activity.
90° – 105°	Sunstroke, heat cramps and heat exhaustion possible with prolonged exposure and/or physical activity.
80° – 90°	Fatigue possible with prolonged exposure and/or physical activity.

*Source: National Oceanic and Atmospheric Administration, National Weather Service/Federal Emergency Management Agency/American Red Cross. *Heat Wave* (brochure). NOAA/PA 85001.

Make Dew

Topic
Condensation: dew point temperature

Key Questions
1. When does water vapor turn back into liquid water?
2. How can air temperature and dew point temperature help us predict the weather?

Focus
Students will measure the water temperature when condensation forms on a can, the dew point. They will also make and use a broken-line graph, comparing air and dew point temperatures, to discover patterns and predict weather conditions.

Guiding Documents
Project 2061 Benchmarks
• *When liquid water disappears, it turns into a gas (vapor) in the air and can reappear as a liquid when cooled, or as a solid if cooled below the freezing point of water. Clouds and fog are made of tiny droplets of water.*
• *Graphical display of numbers may make it possible to spot patterns that are not otherwise obvious, such as comparative size and trends.*

NRC Standards
• *Simple instruments, such as magnifiers, thermometers, and rulers, provide more information than scientists obtain using only their senses.*
• *Materials can exist in different states—solid, liquid, and gas. Some common materials, such as water, can be changed from one state to another by heating or cooling.*
• *Weather changes from day to day and over the seasons. Weather can be described by measurable quantities, such as temperature, wind direction and speed, and precipitation.*

NCTM Standards 2000*
• *Select and apply appropriate standard units and tools to measure length, area, volume, weight, time, temperature, and the size of angles*
• *Collect data using observations, surveys, and experiments*
• *Represent data using tables and graphs such as line plots, bar graphs, and line graphs*

Math
Measurement
  temperature
Graphing
  broken-line
Data analysis

Science
Earth science
  meteorology
    water cycle

Integrated Processes
Observing
Collecting and recording data
Comparing and contrasting
Interpreting data
Relating
Predicting

Materials
Fruit punch and water
Ice cubes
Cups to hold ice cubes
Shiny tin cans, labels removed
Straws or craft sticks for stirring
Soapy water and towels
Thermometers

Background Information
Evaporation, Condensation, and Dew Point
    Evaporation and condensation, together with precipitation, are constantly cycling water between Earth and atmosphere. In warmer temperatures, water molecules move more quickly, allowing them to break their bonds and escape from the surface of the liquid. Liquid water becomes water vapor, a gas, as it evaporates into the air. In cooler temperatures, water vapor molecules slow down enough to bond and condense back into water (liquid) or ice (solid). The condensation may be in the form of fog, clouds, dew, frost, or mist.
    The temperature at which water vapor condenses into liquid is called the dew point temperature and varies with weather conditions. Temperatures at or below freezing (0°C or 32°F) may cause water vapor to condense directly into frost or ice. This is called the frost point temperature.

Dew point is a measure of humidity; the higher the dew point temperature, the more moisture is in the air. The dew point temperature can never be higher than the air temperature.

Patterns and Predictions

The spread between air temperature and dew point temperature can indicate weather conditions. The smaller the gap between these two temperatures, the higher the relative humidity. If the temperatures are equal, the relative humidity is 100%. If the two temperatures are close or the same, the weather will likely be misty, foggy, or rainy.

Dew is more likely on clear nights than cloudy nights. Clouds keep heat energy from leaving the lower atmosphere and temperatures tend to cool less. On clear nights, the heat energy escapes into space. The ground becomes cooler and cools the air next to it. If the air reaches the dew point temperature, dew or fog will form.

Children and the Concept of Condensation

Air is invisible; so is water vapor. With evaporation, we do not see the water rise into the air. We only see the results, disappearing water puddles or drying clothes. When observing condensation, we see the reappearing water but its source, the water vapor in the air, is invisible. This makes it more difficult for children to understand, all the more reason for them to begin observing and thinking about this process.

The important ideas children should gain from this activity are 1) water vapor can condense into liquid water, 2) dew point temperature varies, and 3) air and dew point temperatures which are close together indicate that misty, foggy, or rainy weather is likely.

Management

1. While it is desirable to perform this investigation outdoors, it may also be done indoors. An outdoor setting reflects the actual weather while an indoor setting reflects a more controlled environment, often with lower relative humidity.

2. Dew point temperature should be taken twice, each during different weather conditions. If your weather changes quickly, this might be possible at different times on the same day. More likely, it will need to be done a day or more apart. Or consider comparing the indoor with the outdoor environment.

3. Students can gather tin cans, preferably with smooth surfaces, several days prior to doing the activity. Because students will be tasting the condensation that forms on the can, it is important that the cans first be washed in soapy water. They also need to be completely dry.

4. Punch is used the first time so students can discover that the liquid that forms on the outside of the can does not come from the inside of the can. The second time, water can be used.

5. The same thermometer may be used for both air and dew point temperatures but it must be dry to take air temperature. Two thermometers with the same readings can also be used.

6. Remind students that air temperature should be taken in the shade and fingers should not touch the thermometer bulb.

7. It is helpful for one person to hold the thermometer against the interior side of the can while another person stirs.

8. Groups of two or three are recommended.

Procedure

Part One

1. Introduce the activity by asking questions such as, "Have you ever looked out the window in the morning and noticed the grass is wet? From where do you think that water comes?" Gather student responses. Explain that dew is what the class will be investigating today.

2. Distribute a tin can to each group. Instruct one group member to breathe on the can and then rub a finger where he or she breathed. What did you feel? [dampness or wetness] How does this compare to the tin can before breathing on it? [It was dry.]

3. Give each group *Part One* and have students record what they felt.

4. Have students read the first four directions, gather materials, perform the investigation, and record data. Remind them to wait for the thermometer to stabilize before reading. Weather words might include rainy, clear and cold, sunny and hot, foggy, cloudy, etc.

5. Instruct students to continue observing the can, noticing the film turning into droplets as more liquid collects. Have them rub their fingers on the can and taste the liquid. Does it taste like punch or water? [water] This should help dispel a naive conception that the punch is somehow oozing through the can. From where do you think the water came? [water vapor in the air]

6. Record observations. Have students start a list of examples of condensation.

7. On a day with contrasting weather, repeat the activity. Since students do not need to repeat the taste test, use water this time instead of punch.

8. Dew point temperature is placed directly below "present weather" on the station model, but is not included in our modified version because of the difficulty of continually replicating the dew point measurements.

Part Two: Patterns and Predictions
1. Give students the table and graph labeled *Part Two, Patterns.* Point out that some data are already under the graph. Instruct them to use the table to plot the air and dew point temperature lines, each in a different color. Tell students to connect the points in the key to make color-coded lines.
2. Have students shade the area between the two broken lines to help them focus on the varying gaps between the two temperatures.
3. Encourage students to study the graph and the data below it, looking for patterns and relationships. After discussion within their groups, have them record their discoveries. Then discuss as a class.
4. Distribute the *Part Two, Predictions* graph. Direct students to shade the region between the two plotted lines. Based on the graph, have students predict the likely weather conditions and general relative humidity pattern for the hours given. Discuss.

Actual conditions reported by the National Weather Service:

Fresno, California
May 28, 1998

Time	Weather	Relative Humidity
9 A.M.	fair	54%
10 A.M.	mostly clear	49%
11 A.M.	mostly clear	48%
12 noon	mostly cloudy	41%
1 P.M.	mostly clear	36%
2 P.M.	mostly clear	32%
3 P.M.	mostly clear	39%
4 P.M.	mostly clear	36%
5 P.M.	cloudy	75%
6 P.M.	light rain	89%
7 P.M.	cloudy	90%
8 P.M.	cloudy	80%
9 P.M.	light rain	86%
10 P.M.	cloudy	74%
11 P.M.	partly cloudy	80%
12 mid.	fair	89%

Discussion
Part One
1. How did the outside of the can change? [dry, then dull film, then droplets of water]
2. From where does this water come? [the water vapor in the air] How did the water vapor get into the air? [Water evaporated into the air.]
3. Does the dew point temperature ever change? [Yes] How do you know? [Because we had different dew point temperatures in our two investigations.] How could you gather further proof? [Check the daily weather reports on television or on weather websites.]
4. What examples of condensation have you seen? [morning dew or frost, fog or other clouds, steam from a cooking pot, breath in cold weather, etc.]

 Journal prompt: It is very cold and several people are in your car. Why do the car windows "fog up?" [warm moisture from people's breath meets the cool air inside the car, causing condensation on the windows]

Part Two: Patterns and Predictions
1. Which of the following is true? Which is most likely? Dew point temperature can be higher than air temperature. [no]
   Dew point temperature can be the same as the air temperature. [yes]
   Dew point temperature can be lower than the air temperature. [yes, most likely]
   (To reach these conclusions, students may need to gather further data from weather websites or other sources.)
2. What are likely weather conditions when the dew point and air temperatures are close together? [There will be some kind of moist weather—mist, fog, rain, etc. The smaller the gap in temperatures, the higher the relative humidity. When the temperatures are equal, the relative humidity will be 100%.]
3. *Predictions graph:* What weather conditions were likely during these hours? [The weather was probably fair and relative humidity not too high the first part of the day. Around 5 P.M., there was probably some mist, fog, or rain that continued through the evening. The relative humidity was quite high.]

Extensions

1. Make additional broken-line graphs of air and dew point temperatures by having students gather their own data from a National Weather Service station website. Many have a page with hourly data (sometimes identified as Metar) from the past 48 hours or so.

2. Discuss when condensation becomes a problem. [mildew and mold on walls and in crevices, steam on the bathroom mirror, etc.]

3. Use air and dew point temperatures to find the relative humidity. A relative humidity table using these temperatures will be needed. Check the Internet.

Curriculum Correlation

Literature

Read the Paul Bunyan story, *The Winter of the Blue Snow*, found in a variety of books. This tall tale tells of a very cold winter where spoken words froze in the air. While water vapor usually condenses into liquid water (dew point), very cold temperatures will cause the water vapor to condense directly into ice or frost (frost point).

Connections

Both evaporation and condensation are continually taking place. When the sun's heat energy increases, the rate of evaporation quickens. When the air cools, condensation is more prevalent; the water vapor molecules' constant motion slows and more of them condense back into liquid or solid form as dew, frost, or clouds. Condensation is greatest, given the amount of moisture in the air, when the air temperature cools to the dew point temperature.

From observations of dew and an introduction to dew point temperature, we move to several investigations of clouds. Just how are clouds born?

Make Dew

Part One

Breathe on a tin can. Rub your finger over the can. What do you feel?

1. Wash the tin can in soapy water, rinse, and dry it.
2. Fill the can two-thirds full of liquid and insert a thermometer.
3. Add one ice cube at a time, stirring constantly, until the surface of the can starts to dull. This means the *dew point* has been reached.
4. Take the dew point temperature, keeping the thermometer bulb in the liquid.

Weather

Day/Time _____

Air Temperature _____

Dew Point Temp. _____

Continue to observe the can. Describe what you see.

Does dew point temperature ever change? Repeat under different weather conditions.

Weather

Day/Time _____

Air Temperature _____

Dew Point Temp. _____

What examples of *condensation* have you seen?

Make Dew

Use this data table to make a broken-line graph of the air temperature and the dew point temperature.

Indianapolis, Indiana
July 16, 1998

Time	Air Temp. (°F)	Dew Pt. Temp. (°F)
2 A.M.	68	67
3 A.M.	68	67
4 A.M.	68	67
5 A.M.	68	68
6 A.M.	68	67
7 A.M.	69	68
8 A.M.	72	69
9 A.M.	77	69
10 A.M.	80	70
11 A.M.	81	70
12 noon	84	70
1 P.M.	84	69
2 P.M.	88	70
3 P.M.	86	67
4 P.M.	87	67
5 P.M.	87	66
6 P.M.	86	63
7 P.M.	84	64

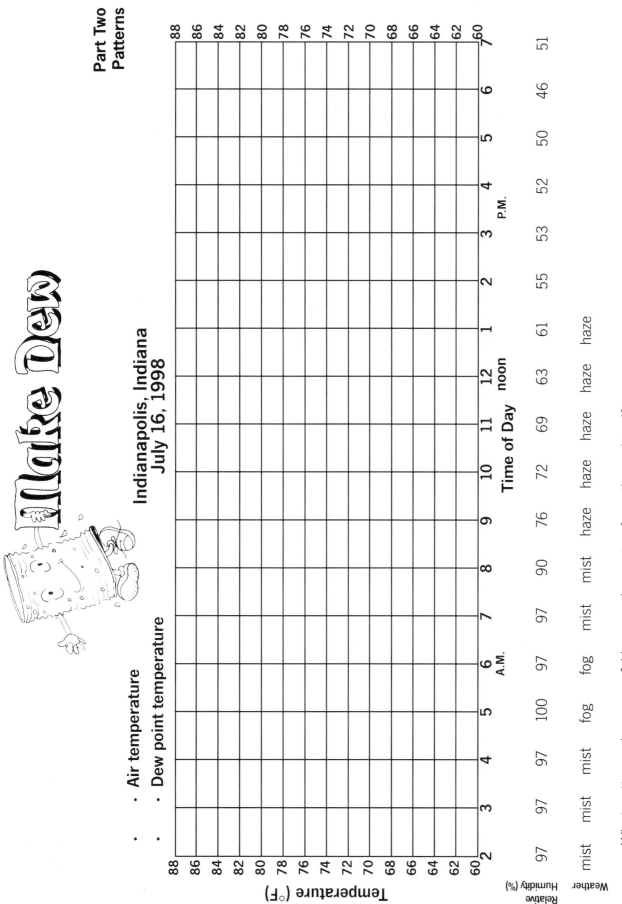

Make Dew

**Part Two
Patterns**

Indianapolis, Indiana
July 16, 1998

- Air temperature
- Dew point temperature

Temperature (°F) (axis: 60, 62, 64, 66, 68, 70, 72, 74, 76, 78, 80, 82, 84, 86, 88)

Time of Day

Time of Day	2	3	4	5	6 A.M.	7	8	9	10	11	12 noon	1	2	3	4 P.M.	5	6	7
Relative Humidity (%)	97	97	97	100	97	97	90	76	72	69	63	61	55	53	52	50	46	51
Weather	mist	mist	mist	fog	fog	mist	mist	haze	haze	haze	haze	haze						

What patterns do you see? How are the parts of weather related?

Make Dew

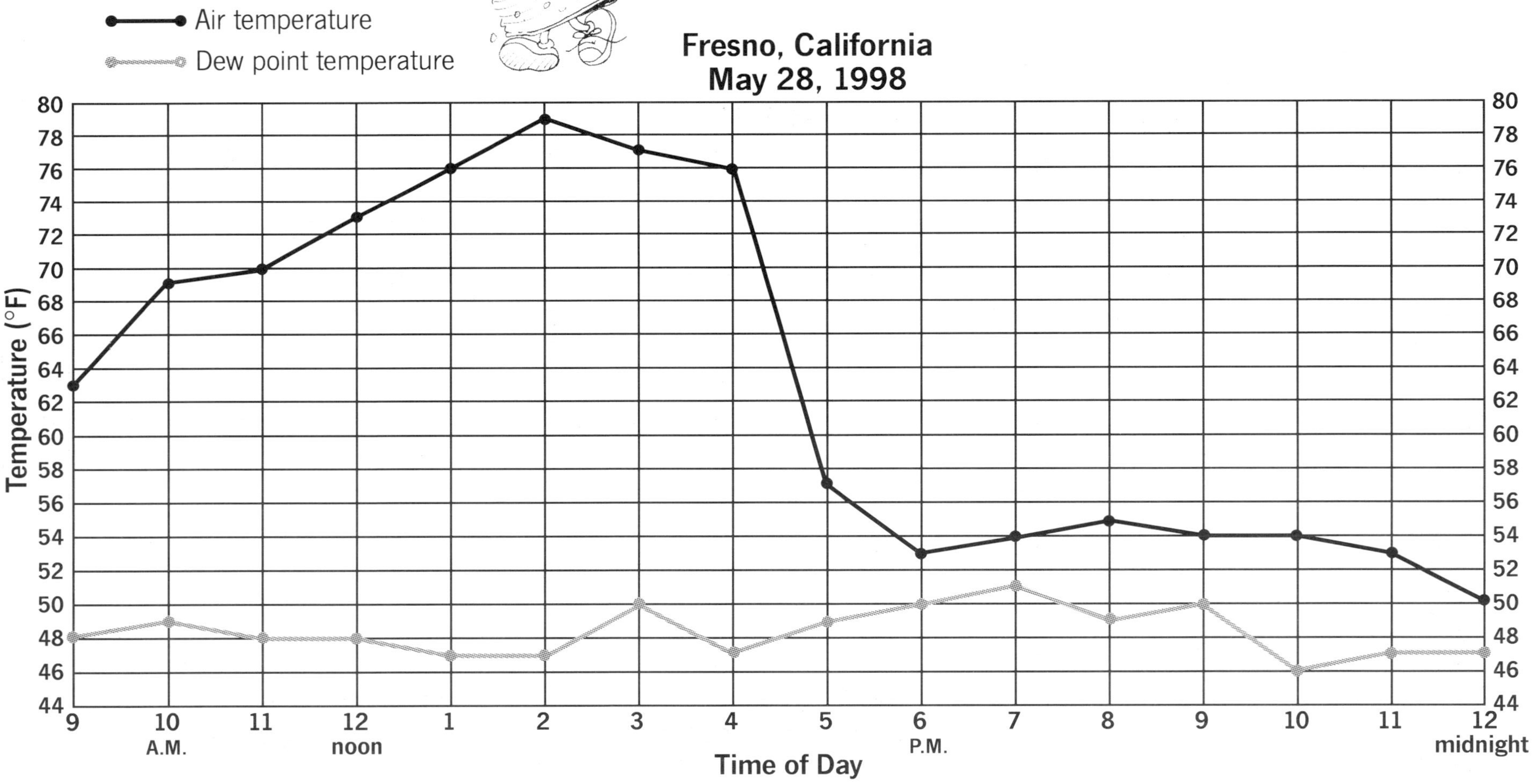

Part 2
Predictions

Fresno, California
May 28, 1998

— Air temperature
— Dew point temperature

Temperature (°F)

Time of Day

Study the graph. What weather conditions were likely during these hours?

How would you describe the relative humidity at different times of the day?

Topic
Clouds: condensation nuclei

Key Question
How does a cloud form?

Focus
Students will observe how water vapor collects on salt grains, simulating the role of condensation nuclei in the formation of clouds.

Guiding Documents
Project 2061 Benchmark
• *When liquid water disappears, it turns into a gas (vapor) in the air and can reappear as a liquid when cooled, or as a solid if cooled below the freezing point of water. Clouds and fog are made of tiny droplets of water.*

NRC Standard
• *Clouds, formed by the condensation of water vapor, affect weather and climate.*

Science
Earth science
  meteorology
    water cycle

Integrated Processes
Observing
Comparing and contrasting
Relating

Materials
For each group:
  black or gray film canister lid
  waterproof saucer
  transparent jar or cup
  water
  salt
  hand lens

Management
Small groups of two or three allow for closer observation.

Background Information
Clouds are formed when water vapor condenses on tiny particles in the atmosphere, called condensation nuclei. Very tiny particles of salt from sea spray, much smaller than the grains of salt being observed, are among the nuclei that collect water. In fact, salt is the primary condensation nuclei in the atmosphere over the oceans. Other nuclei include dust, smoke, volcanic ash, and even pollutants.

In this activity, the water evaporating inside the jar is drawn to the salt grains because salt is hygroscopic. This means it is able to absorb water from the air. The water vapor condenses on the salt and the grains dissolve in the water.

Procedure
1. Have students follow the directions listed on the task card and discuss the results.
2. Encourage students to share cloud experiences they have had (see *Make Your Own Cloud*).
3. Perform the pint jar activity as students observe.
   • What do you observe when the balloon skin is pushed down? [The air in the jar is clearer.]
   • What do you observe when the balloon skin is pulled up? [A cloud forms. (As the pressure decreases, evaporation increases. It takes less energy for the water molecules to break free of the surface and become water vapor.)]
   • On what kind of particles is the water vapor condensing? [smoke]

Discussion
1. How do the salt grains change? [At the beginning, they are white and almost shaped like a cube. They become more and more transparent. Then they dissolve in the water beads that have formed.]
2. Where did the water come from? [The water from the saucer evaporated into the air inside the cup. Then the salt grains absorbed it.]
3. How is our observation like what happens when clouds form in the atmosphere? [The water vapor in the air collects and condenses on tiny particles of smoke, sea spray (salt), dust, etc.]
4. How is our observation different? [The grains of salt are much, much bigger than the particles around which water condenses in the atmosphere.]
5. Usually we look up at clouds. Have you ever been above a cloud? [in a plane; in the hills, looking down on a foggy valley] Describe your experience.

Connections
Clouds are one form of condensation. When moist, rising air cools to the dew point temperature, water vapor molecules slow down, bond, and grow around tiny particles such as salt or smoke, becoming visible as clouds. The amount of sky blanketed by clouds has a significant effect on weather. We will learn more about this and also practice estimating sky cover in the next activity.

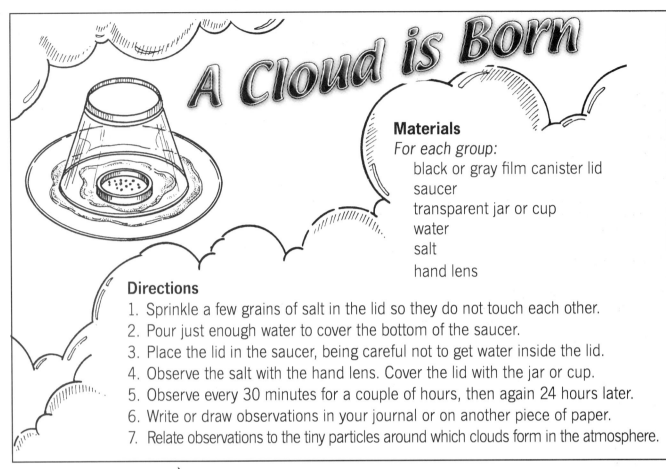

A Cloud is Born

Materials

For each group:
- black or gray film canister lid
- saucer
- transparent jar or cup
- water
- salt
- hand lens

Directions
1. Sprinkle a few grains of salt in the lid so they do not touch each other.
2. Pour just enough water to cover the bottom of the saucer.
3. Place the lid in the saucer, being careful not to get water inside the lid.
4. Observe the salt with the hand lens. Cover the lid with the jar or cup.
5. Observe every 30 minutes for a couple of hours, then again 24 hours later.
6. Write or draw observations in your journal or on another piece of paper.
7. Relate observations to the tiny particles around which clouds form in the atmosphere.

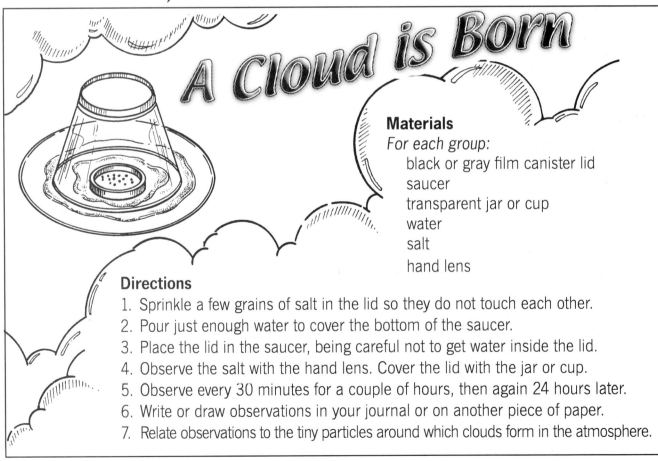

A Cloud is Born

Materials

For each group:
- black or gray film canister lid
- saucer
- transparent jar or cup
- water
- salt
- hand lens

Directions
1. Sprinkle a few grains of salt in the lid so they do not touch each other.
2. Pour just enough water to cover the bottom of the saucer.
3. Place the lid in the saucer, being careful not to get water inside the lid.
4. Observe the salt with the hand lens. Cover the lid with the jar or cup.
5. Observe every 30 minutes for a couple of hours, then again 24 hours later.
6. Write or draw observations in your journal or on another piece of paper.
7. Relate observations to the tiny particles around which clouds form in the atmosphere.

A Cloud is Born

Make Your Own Cloud

When it is hot...

When it is cold...

In a pint jar...

(Have an adult demonstrate.)

1. Cut off the neck of a *9-inch balloon.* Stretch the remaining skin over the *glass pint jar* to make sure it fits. Remove the skin.
2. Fill the jar about 2 cm deep with *hot water.* Swish the water around the jar to warm the sides. Pour out all but a small amount, 15 mL (1 tablespoon) or so.
3. Light a *match* and drop it into the jar.
4. Quickly cover the jar with the balloon skin. Put a piece of *dark construction paper* behind the jar for contrasting background.
5. Push against the balloon skin. Then pull on the balloon skin.

What do you observe?

Topic
Station model: cloud cover

Key Question
How much of the sky is covered by clouds?

Focus
After practicing with a paper area model, students will estimate the amount of sky covered by clouds. They will choose the appropriate international meteorological symbol to represent their observation on the station model.

Guiding Documents
Project 2061 Benchmark
* *When liquid water disappears, it turns into a gas (vapor) in the air and can reappear as a liquid when cooled, or as a solid if cooled below the freezing point of water. Clouds and fog are made of tiny droplets of water.*

NRC Standards
* *The sun, moon, stars, clouds, birds, and airplanes all have properties, locations, and movements that can be observed and described.*
* *Clouds, formed by the condensation of water vapor, affect weather and climate.*

NCTM Standards 2000*
* *Develop strategies for estimating the perimeters, areas, and volumes of irregular shapes*
* *Collect data using observations, surveys, and experiments*

Math
Estimation
    area
    percents
Spatial sense

Science
Earth science
    meteorology
        water cycle

Integrated Processes
Observing
Collecting and recording data
Comparing and contrasting

Materials
9" x 12" blue and white construction paper,
    one of each per student
Scissors
Glue

Background Information
One of the weather conditions noted by meteorologists is the amount of sky covered by clouds. Temperature fluctuations on Earth are determined partly by clouds. A very cloudy sky reflects more of the sun's heat energy back into space, keeping Earth temperatures cooler. At the same time, heavy cloud cover traps the heat energy already absorbed by the Earth, moderating temperature change between day and night. Conversely, a lack of clouds allows heat energy to flow freely to and from the Earth, causing greater temperature extremes between day and night.

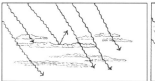 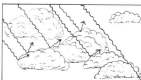

Thin clouds	Thick clouds

As of 1996, meteorologists around the world use a common set of six symbols to report sky cover as shown on the *Sky Cover Chart*. Sky cover estimates are subjective, dependent on the judgment of the observer. Meteorologists use octas, which are *not* based on dividing the sky into eight equal sections, to determine the amount of sky cover.

Clear	no clouds
Few	0-2 octas
Scattered	3-4 octas
Broken	5-7 octas
Overcast	8 octas
Obscured	cannot be observed

Because octas require a complex knowledge of weather and mathematics, percents are a more accessible way for students of all ages to think about sky cover. The sky, all 360 degrees of it from horizon to horizon, appears hemispherical. The circle model, already familiar through the use of circle graphs, represents 100% of this hemisphere, flattened. The percents in the *Sky Cover Chart* are somewhat arbitrary, since the octas meterologists use are not directly equivalent to percents.

Estimating the amount of cloud cover is a part-to-whole comparison involving informal area measurement. The challenge is that most clouds are not neatly joined together in one part of the sky but are scattered about. The brain has to take into account the spaces between the clouds when making a judgment. Nor do clouds have regular, congruent shapes.

The sky cover symbol forms the base around which a station model is built. This is a graphic model of weather information for a specific location, seen on some surface weather maps. Each piece of data is assigned a particular place in relation to the central sky cover symbol. See the *Station Model* activity for further information.

sky cover

Management

1. Make copies of the circle, representing the sky, on blue construction paper and copies of the sectioned circle, representing the clouds, on white construction paper.
2. When making sky observations, caution students to not look directly at the sun.

Procedure

1. Take the class outdoors to a location where as much of the sky as possible is visible in all directions. Ask students to estimate how much of the total sky is covered by clouds—all clouds. Gather their answers in whatever form they are phrased: as generalizations (most of the sky, just a little, etc.), as fractions (about one-half, three-fourths, etc.), or as percentages (10%, 50%, etc.)
2. Back indoors, discuss how easy or hard it was to make an estimate.
3. Explain that the amount of sky cover is one of the observations made by meteorologists, along with temperature, wind direction and speed, etc. Announce that the class is going to practice estimations by making and using some paper sky models.
4. Distribute the construction paper circles (see *Management 1)* and have students cut them out. Direct attention to the sectioned circle and ask, "Into how

many parts is this circle divided?" [10] "If the circle represents the whole sky (100%), what percent is one part?" [10%] "What percent are six parts?" [60%]

5. Suggest that each student choose a group of parts, at least one but not more than nine, that will represent clouds on his or her sky model. Have students cut out this group and turn it over, since the section lines serve no further purpose and may be distracting.
6. Instruct students to cut the white paper into irregular pieces and glue them inside the blue circle in any configuration they wish (closely bunched, spread out, or a combination), so long as the pieces do not overlap. On the back, ask them to write the percent of clouds they chose.
7. Hold up different sky models and have the class estimate the amount of sky cover.
8. Give students the *Sky Cover Chart* and direct them to relate their estimates to one of the six categories used by meteorologists.
9. Have students make a set of the six sky cover symbols out of black and white construction paper to use for the school station model. Use the circle template in the *Station Model* activity or draw your own, 10 cm in diameter or larger. Additional sets can be made if the class will be displaying station models for other cities in the country and/or world.

Discussion

1. How easy was it to estimate the amount of sky cover? (It depends upon the conditions. Clear and obscured skies aren't difficult to identify. The challenge lies in determining in which of four categories partially cloudy skies belong.)
2. Are all our percent estimates alike? (Probably not, since sky cover is a subjective observation.) Do we agree on the category in which today's sky cover belongs? (Probably, because each category spans a range of percents.)
3. Why do you think meteorologists take note of cloud cover? [It affects air temperature—how much heat energy gets through to or is trapped on the Earth's surface and also the amount of contrast between daytime and nighttime temperatures.]
4. When do you pay attention to cloud cover?

* Reprinted with permission from *Principles and Standards for School Mathematics,* 2000 by the National Council of Teachers of Mathematics. All rights reserved.

Connections

Observations of cloud cover are tied to two big ideas. First, the flow of heat energy from the sun to Earth and back into space happens freely with a lack of clouds and is impeded with the presence of significant cloud cover. Second, the formation of clouds is evidence of the condensation part of the water cycle.

The use of the sky cover symbols on the station model, when linked to temperature and other weather data, should help students see cause and effect. Once students have learned to estimate the amount of cloud coverage, they are ready to delve into the three main cloud types in *Sky Watch.*

Clouds

Sky Cover

Sky

Sky Cover

⦿	Clear	No clouds
⦶	Few	present but < 10%
◑	Scattered	10 - 50%
◖	Broken	50 - 90%
●	Overcast	more than 90%
⊗	Obscured	**cannot be observed** (possibly fog, haze, blowing snow, smoke, volcanic ash, dust, sand, sea spray, heavy rain, or heavy snow)

Sky Watch

Topic
Three basic clouds

Key Questions
1. How do clouds compare?
2. How are clouds and weather related?

Focus
Students will observe the three basic types of clouds—cirrus, cumulus, and stratus—and begin to relate them to certain kinds of weather.

Guiding Documents
Project 2061 Benchmarks
- *When liquid water disappears, it turns into a gas (vapor) in the air and can reappear as a liquid when cooled, or as a solid if cooled below the freezing point of water. Clouds and fog are made of tiny droplets of water.*
- *Keep records of their investigations and observations and not change the records later.*

NRC Standards
- *Materials can exist in different states—solid, liquid, and gas. Some common materials, such as water, can be changed from one state to another by heating or cooling.*
- *The sun, moon, stars, clouds, birds, and airplanes all have properties, locations, and movements that can be observed and described.*
- *Clouds, formed by the condensation of water vapor, affect weather and climate.*

Science
Earth science
   meteorology
      water cycle

Integrated Processes
Observing
Collecting and recording data
Comparing and contrasting
Classifying
Relating

Materials
Pictures of cirrus, cumulus, and stratus clouds
   (see *Management 1*)
Transparent tape

Background Information
Cloud formation and the water cycle

   Water evaporates into the air, becoming water vapor, a gas. As the moist air rises, it cools by 2.8°C (5.4°F) for about every 300 meters (1000 feet). When the rising air cools to the dew point temperature (which varies), water vapor condenses on tiny particles in the air—dust, volcanic ash, salt from ocean spray, pollen, even pollution particles. These water droplets or ice crystals may become of sufficient size and quantity to be visible as clouds. Sunlight bounces off them, scattering the light and making the clouds appear white.

   Condensation continues as long as the air continues to rise, causing the cloud droplets to grow. If the droplets become large and heavy enough, they fall to the Earth as rain, snow, or some other form of precipitation.

   Clouds formed by moist, rising air may produce rain on the windward side of the mountains. But once the clouds cross the ridge, the air begins to descend and warm, causing evaporation and a comparatively drier climate on the leeward side.

   Generally, clouds are formed when rising air cools to the dew point. However, cooling air, normally near the surface at night, can result in fog or low stratus clouds. Clouds also form when warm air moves over a cooler surface, for example, when warm air over an ocean or lake moves over cooled land at night.

Clouds' effects on Earth

   Clouds help regulate the temperature of the Earth. Thick clouds act like a blanket, reflecting the sun's rays back into space as well as trapping heat energy on Earth. When it is cloudless, the sun's heat energy radiates freely to the Earth during the day and escapes freely from the Earth at night; this generally causes a greater contrast between daytime and nighttime temperatures.

   Clouds also replenish the Earth with water, keeping the water cycle in motion. While clouds do not always bring precipitation, there must be clouds for rain, snow, or other forms of precipitation to take place.

Types of clouds

   Clouds are classified both by their appearance and by their altitude above the Earth. While there are ten major types of clouds identified by meteorologists, they can be overwhelming for the beginner at whatever age. It is most important to first become familiar with three types of clouds—cirrus, cumulus, and stratus.

The other clouds are forms or combinations of these three and are addressed in the activity, *Cloud Combos.*

Cloud Type	Description	Height	Related Weather	Forecast
Cirrus	curls, thin and wispy, mare's tails; ice crystals	above 6 km (20,000 ft)	fair	if warm front coming, can be first sign of storm (may evolve into nimbostratus)
Cumulus	heap or pile with flat base, detached, like cotton puffs; water droplets	1-5 km (3000-16,500 ft)	fair	if appears in moist, rising morning air, expect stormy weather; if appears in afternoon, expect fair weather
Stratus	smooth, even layers, stretched out, includes fog; water droplets	below 2 km (6500 ft)	overcast	------

Clouds, weather, and forecasting

Clouds are one of several guides as to what weather is coming, although weather doesn't always follow a set pattern and can change very quickly.

If there are no clouds in the sky, the weather will be fair. It means the air is dry; there is not enough moisture in the air for clouds to form.

The weather may be fair when cirrus clouds first appear, but they are often the first sign of a coming warm front. As the front gets closer, the clouds typically become thicker and lower stratus clouds. The stratus clouds may become dark (nimbostratus) and produce precipitation.

Cumulus clouds may appear as the weather clears. If a cold front moves in, they become taller and darker thunderclouds (cumulonimbus) and can produce heavy rain over a short period of time.

Management

1. Sources for cloud pictures include books, videos, posters, and websites. Sets of Cloud Charts, like the one with this book, are available from AIMS. Other pictures are available from: Cloud Chart, Inc., P.O. Box 21298, Charleston, SC 29413.

2. To record cloud observations, each student will first need to assemble the layered booklet. You may wish to cut the pages to size beforehand. If you wish to use less paper, students can make their own recording page with the three cloud types listed on the left (each allowed a third of a page) and the following headings:

   Date/Time   Present Weather   Weather That Follows

3. The length of this activity is dependent on nature; data gathering could take several weeks. Consider using this activity as an introduction to the weather unit.

Observation times should be based on the variety of clouds that appear, not on a certain time every day. With rapidly changing weather, two or more observations can be made in a single day. If clouds and weather remain the same, only one observation might be made in an entire week. Aim for at least three sightings of each type of cloud.

4. While looking at the sky, never look directly at the sun as it can damage eyesight.

5. As students observe clouds, they will probably have all kinds of questions. Keep a list of their questions to use for further exploration and to evaluate their understanding of clouds and the water cycle.

6. The goal of this activity is to become acquainted with the three basic types of clouds and how they relate to the weather and, in the process, strengthen observation skills. Previous experience and continuing observation both contribute to the construction of learning. The need to learn about more specific cloud groups (see *Cloud Combos*) should arise naturally, out of increasingly detailed observations and questions that are posed.

Procedure

1. Ask the students: "Have you ever laid back on the lawn and looked at the clouds? Did you see any shaped like animals? ... like something else?" Explain that students will be looking more closely at clouds in the coming days.

2. Use pictures to introduce the look of the three main types of clouds—stratus, cumulus, and cirrus. Give just enough information for identification, saving the relative heights of clouds for student observation.

3. Distribute the booklet pages. Have students assemble and staple the layers together.

4. Take the class outside, reminding them to never look directly at the sun. Have students describe how the clouds look (color, shape, etc.) and identify them. Ask students to describe the present weather subjectively—cold/warm, fair/overcast, windy/calm, sticky/dry, etc. Though not essential, quantitative measurements may also be taken.

5. Return indoors and instruct students to record the date, time, and present weather.

6. Have students record the weather that follows their initial cloud observations, usually between six and 24 hours later. It is possible that as they are recording the weather which follows one cloud observation, they will also be making a new entry for a different type of cloud. Guide them through this task as needed.

7. Repeat cloud and weather observations over time until there are three or more for each type of cloud. Patience is important.

8. Discuss what has been observed and explain how clouds are part of the water cycle. Close with the book, *Small Cloud*, listed in *Curriculum Correlation.*

Discussion

1. What kind of cloud(s) did we see today? How did you make your decision? (Student answers should reflect on how the look of the cloud related to the cloud pictures they had been shown or the difficulty they had deciding when the cloud had features from two groups. They may begin to feel the need for additional cloud groups, such as stratocumulus, to describe what they are observing. That would make a natural lead-in to *Cloud Combos.*)

2. What other observations did you make about clouds? [Their heights are different: cirrus clouds are very high, cumulus clouds are lower but tall, and stratus clouds are the lowest. (Other comments on color or shape may be offered.)]

3. As you look at the whole sky, about how much of it do you think is covered by clouds? (Responses may be expressed as fractions—none, $\frac{1}{4}$, $\frac{1}{2}$, $\frac{3}{4}$, all—or as the percents practiced in *Sky Cover.*)

4. How do clouds fit into the water cycle? [Water evaporates into the air. When the temperature of moist, rising air cools to the dew point, the water vapor in the air condenses into tiny droplets that form clouds. If the water or ice droplets keep collecting and become large enough, they fall to Earth as rain, snow, or other kinds of precipitation.]

5. What kind of present weather seems to be related to each cloud? [cirrus—fair; cumulus—fair; stratus—overcast] Were the results the same time after time? (While broad generalizations may be made, there are stronger links between weather and more specific cloud types. See the *Cloud Table* in the activity, *Cloud Combos.*)

6. What weather pattern seems to follow certain clouds? [Forecasting based on clouds alone is insufficient. Cirrus clouds may signal coming stormy weather or fair weather may continue. Cumulus clouds may precede or follow a storm. Stratus clouds may or may not indicate any change in weather.]

7. Now that we have been observing clouds for awhile, what are you curious about?

 Journal prompt: Write a poem about clouds or a particular kind of cloud.
- four-line poem with or without a rhyming pattern (ABAB, AABB, ABCA, etc.)
- haiku (see the supporting page)
- simile using *like* or *as*
    A cumulus cloud is like a giant's pillow.
    Stratus clouds spread like a blanket over the Earth.
    Cirrus clouds are as thin as wisps of breath.

Extensions

1. Have students use mirrors to informally observe the direction and speed with which clouds may be moving. (Note: 3" x 5" mirrors are available from AIMS.) Directions—north, south, east, and west—may be written directly on the mirror with an overhead pen (a) or on a piece of construction paper to which the mirror is attached (b).

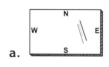 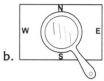

a. b.

Set the mirror on a flat surface, orientate it to north, and follow an identifiable part of a cloud as it moves. Name the directions the cloud is coming from and going to, for example, northwest to southeast. Is it moving slowly or quickly?

2. Do the cloud section of the *Station Model* activity. It deals with the amount of sky covered by clouds and optional cloud identification.

Curriculum Correlation

Literature

Ariane. *Small Cloud.* Walker and Company. New York. 1996. (An endearing tale of the birth of a cloud, its travels, and how it eventually feeds the Earth with rain, completing a journey through the water cycle.)

Markert, Jenny. *Clouds.* Creative Education, Inc. Mankato, MN. 1992. (Brief but informative text and gorgeous full-page colored photographs of the three types of clouds and associated weather phenomena. An excellent introduction for elementary students.)

Art

1. For a tactile cloud experience, have students illustrate the look of the three major kinds of clouds using cotton. Guide students in folding a 12" x 18" piece of construction paper in thirds and writing a cloud name in each section. Give them three cotton balls and have students pull them apart to resemble each of the clouds. After gluing the cotton in place, they may wish to draw a scene appropriate to the weather for each cloud.

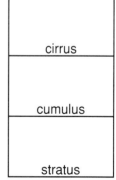

2. Choose appropriate famous pictures with clouds using posters, books, or other media. Some suggestions follow, many of which can be found at
http://sunsite.auc.dk/cgfa/fineart.htm
With students, explore the composition of the pictures (art appreciation) and discuss the clouds depicted.

Paintings
Paul Cezanne (1839-1906), French
House of Dr. Gachet in Auvers

John Constable (1776-1837), British
Wivenhoe Park, Essex, and others

Camille Corot (1796-1875), French
Chartres Cathedral

Gustave Courbet (1819-1877), French
The Calm Sea and *The Wave*

Vincent van Gogh (1853-1890), Dutch
The Starry Night

Edouard Manet (1832-1883), French
Racetrack Near Paris

Claude Monet (1840-1926), French
Terrace at St. Adresse

Georgia O'Keefe (1887-1986), American
Pink Dish and Green Leaves

Rembrandt (1606-1669), Dutch
The Mill

Norman Rockwell (1894-1978), American
Looking Out to Sea (Outward Bound)

Jacob van Ruisdael (approx. 1628-1682), Dutch
Rough Sea, View of Haarlem, and *The Windmill at Wijk bij Duurstede*

John Singer Sargent (1856-1925), American
Oyster Gatherers of Cancale

J.M.W. Turner (1775-1851), British
Fishermen at Sea and others

Jan Vermeer (1632-1675), Dutch
View of Delft

Photographs
Ansel Adams (1902-1984), American
Noon Clouds, Glacier NP
Golden Gate Before the Bridge
Moon and Mount McKinley
Clouds, Kings River Divide, Sierra Nevada
Lake MacDonald, Glacier NP
Big Bend NP
Moon and Clouds
Half Dome and Clouds
and many more

Connections

As moist, rising air cools to the dew point, condensation occurs. The very cold air at high altitudes causes water vapor to condense as ice (cirrus clouds), while at warmer temperatures it condenses as water (stratus and most of cumulus clouds).

Clouds contribute to the unequal heating of the Earth. Heavy cloud cover blocks much of the sun's radiation and keeps heat energy on Earth captive; temperature variations during the 24-hour day are relatively small. In areas with light cloud cover, heat energy moves freely between sun and Earth, causing warmer days and cooler nights.

Some of the artistry of weather is seen in the shapes of clouds. As students appreciate the varied skyscapes, they may feel the need for more specific cloud groups to describe what they are observing, a natural lead-in to *Cloud Combos.*

Sky Watch

What kind of weather seems to be related to each cloud?

To assemble the booklet, cut the three pages.
Fold the cover page and staple the three pages inside.

Use the pages to record three or more observations of each kind of cloud.

- -

Date/Time	Present Weather	Weather That Follows

CIRRUS
(Latin for curl or tuft)

- -

Sky Watch

✂ -

Date/Time	Present Weather	Weather That Follows

CUMULUS
(Latin for heap or pile)

✂ -

91

Sky Watch

- -

Date/Time	Present Weather	Weather That Follows

STRATUS
Latin for stretched out)

_____
fold line

Sky Watch Haiku

A haiku is an unrhymed Japanese poem with 3 short lines and traditionally, though not always, 17 syllables. It often suggests ideas and feelings about nature and refers to a season of the year. Let your observations of clouds inspire you to write a haiku.

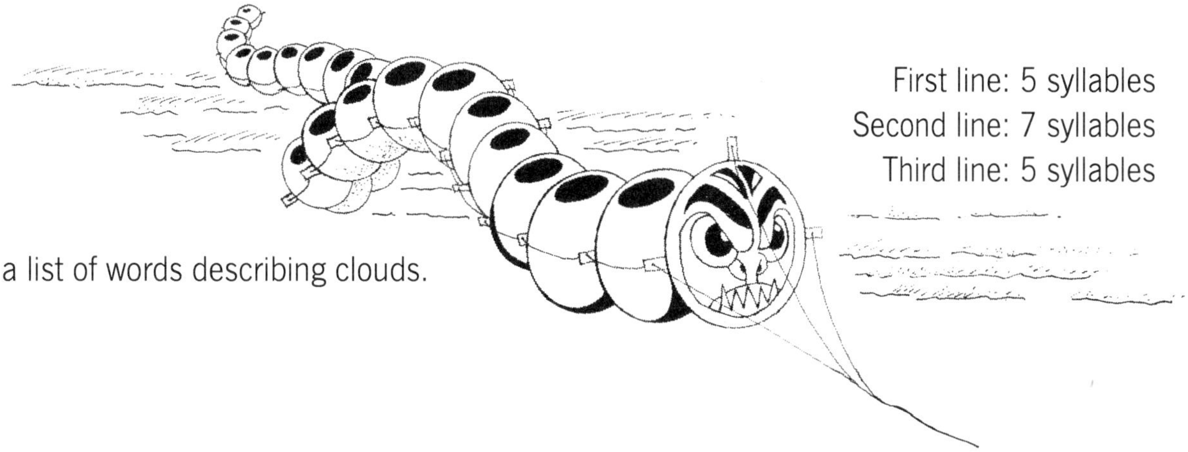

First line: 5 syllables
Second line: 7 syllables
Third line: 5 syllables

Make a list of words describing clouds.

Now try some phrases with 5 to 7 syllables.

_____

_____

_____

_____

Your haiku:

_____

_____

_____

Cloud Combos

Topic
Cloud combinations

Key Question
How do words help us identify and describe clouds?

Focus
Students will use five word cells—cirrus, cumulus, stratus, nimbus, and alto—to form cloud combinations and use their meanings to describe the clouds. Through research, students will find application to the cloud classification system used by meteorologists.

Guiding Documents
Project 2061 Benchmarks
- *When liquid water disappears, it turns into a gas (vapor) in the air and can reappear as a liquid when cooled, or as a solid if cooled below the freezing point of water. Clouds and fog are made of tiny droplets of water.*
- *Buttress their statements with facts found in books, articles, and databases, and identify the sources used and expect others to do the same.*

NRC Standards
- *The sun, moon, stars, clouds, birds, and airplanes all have properties, locations, and movements that can be observed and described.*
- *Clouds, formed by the condensation of water vapor, affect weather and climate.*

Science
Earth science
   meteorology
      water cycle

Literacy/Language Arts
Vocabulary development
Research

Integrated Processes
Observing
Collecting and recording data
Comparing and contrasting
Classifying
Relating

Materials
Sources for cloud research (see *Management 1*)
Scissors (for option A)

Background Information
Clouds

Clouds are made of water or ice particles condensed from water vapor which has evaporated into the air. They belong to the condensation part of the water cycle and, under the right conditions, produce precipitation. In addition to being the source of precipitation, they also help regulate the Earth's temperature. Like a blanket, clouds keep heat energy from escaping the Earth's atmosphere as well as bouncing some of the sun's rays back into space.

Clouds were first classified in 1803. Luke Howard (1772-1864), a British pharmacist with a keen interest in meteorology, named four cloud types—cirrus, which looks like curls; cumulus, which means heap or pile; stratus, from the Latin word for stretched out; and nimbus, rain clouds. At the first International Meteorological Congress in 1874, scientists used Howard's names to develop the cloud classification system of ten genera used today. The ten genera are divided into four groups according to altitude—high (cirrus, cirrocumulus, cirrostratus), middle (altocumulus, altostratus), low (nimbostratus, stratus, stratocumulus), and vertical (cumulus, cumulonimbus). Although their bases are generally at low or middle altitudes, vertical clouds can be tall, sometimes rising above cirrus clouds. See the *Cloud Table* and *Picture Graph* for more information.

The intent of this activity is to help students become aware of cloud groups beyond the big three, as the need for more specific identification arises with continued observation. However, it is better to know the three basic kinds of clouds well than to be overwhelmed by distinctions between the ten cloud groups.

The power of word cells

A word cell is the smallest part of a word that has meaning. Word cells are a powerful means for building vocabulary and understanding. For example, if students have learned that "meter" means "measure," when they see a new word with "meter" in it, they already know it is the measure of something. If they know other word cells like "peri" (around), "therm" (heat), and "alto" (high), they can construct the meaning of perimeter, thermometer, and altimeter.

The names of the ten cloud groups used by meteorologists are all based on five word cells—cirrus, cumulus, stratus, nimbus, and alto—whose meanings, used in combination, are a more natural gateway to cloud awareness than straight memorization of names.

Management

1. Sources for researching cloud types include books, encyclopedias, videos, posters, and websites. Sets of Cloud Charts, like the one with this book, are available from AIMS. Other pictures are available from: Cloud Chart, Inc., P.O. Box 21298, Charleston, SC 29413.

2. Choose which of the two options you wish students to use for organizing data. Option A is more open-ended while option B presents a visual organizational scheme. Each student should record his or her own word combinations but discuss and do research within a small group.

Procedure

1. Read the book, *Willie Whyner, Cloud Designer* (see *Curriculum Correlation*). Explain that, although Willie's clouds were make-believe, there are some real kinds of clouds students have not yet met. They will first be introduced to these clouds through words and word meanings rather than cloud pictures.

2. Distribute either the option A or option B activity page. Have students spend time studying and discussing the five word cells and pictures, as these words are the key to making sense of cloud names.

3. For option A, instruct students to follow the directions, physically moving the word cells together and writing the names on the page. For option B, have students write word combinations in the intersections on the circle.

   You may want to inform students that word cells ending in "-us" are usually changed to "-o" when used as a prefix. Example: cirrus becomes cirro as in cirrostratus, nimbus becomes nimbo, etc. However, you do not need to focus on the spelling or the order of the word combinations at this time.

4. Have students describe how these cloud combinations would look and their general position in the sky, based on word meaning alone.

5. Direct students to find pictures and charts of clouds to confirm which of their cloud combinations are cloud names used by scientists. Spellings and word cell position can be adjusted at this time. For example, nimbocumulus would be changed to cumulonimbus.

   For option A, have students draw a line through word combinations that are not used. For option B, instruct students to put an "x" (or a circle with a slash) through the words and pictures that do not apply.

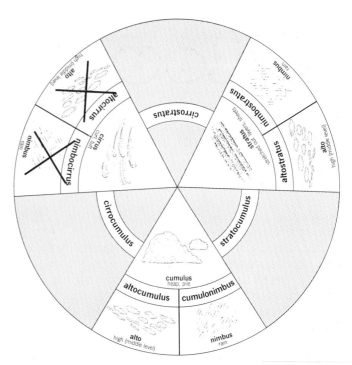

6. Give students the *Cloud Table* and *Picture Graph*. Have them examine the various data: height, kind of particles, and shape.

7. Relate, or have students relate, the part clouds play in the water cycle.

Discussion

1. How do you know you found all the possible word combinations for the clouds? (Encourage students to explain their organizing process.)

2. How does knowing the meanings of words help you describe the clouds? [Nimbostratus, for example, means "rain" and "stretched out." So the cloud has to be dark, rainy, and stretched across the sky.]

3. I wonder if any of these word cells are used in other kinds of words? (Using a dictionary, students will find that a form of *alto*, meaning high, is used in the words altitude and altimeter. Learning the meanings of word cells can be a powerful tool for building vocabulary.)

4. Explain the part clouds play in the water cycle. [They are the condensation part of the water cycle. Water vapor from evaporation condenses on tiny dust or other particles. Sometimes enough water or ice collects so that it falls to Earth as precipitation.]

For those who are ready for more of a challenge:

5. You are observing clouds and identify them as cirrus because they are so high in the sky. How might you know which kind they are—cirrostratus, cirrocumulus, or cirrus? [I would look at the shape. Cirro*stratus* are layered, cirro*cumulus* are puffy, and cirrus look like locks of hair.]

6. You observe some clouds in the stratus family. How might you know which kind they are—stratus, nimbostratus, stratocumulus, altostratus, or cirrostratus? [I would check whether they are layered and puffy, strato*cumulus*, or dark and rainy, *nimbo*stratus. If those descriptions didn't fit, I would look at how high they are in the sky. According to our pictures and table, *cirro*stratus are very high in the sky, *alto*stratus are middle clouds, and regular stratus are low.]

Extensions
1. Add cumulonimbus, because of its importance to weather, to the observation repertoire of cirrus, cumulus, and stratus. Some students may be ready to incorporate other cloud combinations into their observations, but go slowly and gently into this. It is better to learn to identify a few key clouds consistently, than try to identify many different clouds and become confused or frustrated.
2. Optional: Consult *The Audubon Society Field Guide to North American Weather* by David M. Ludlum (Alfred A. Knopf, New York, 1991) or search the Internet for the placement of high, middle, and low clouds on the station model. The symbols are shown in the *Cloud Table*.

Curriculum Correlation
Literature

Lustig, Michael and Esther. *Willy Whyner, Cloud Designer*. Four Winds Press (Macmillan). New York. 1994. (A fantasy about a third-grade boy who makes unusual kinds of clouds. Tongue-in-cheek humor.)

Music

To reinforce linguistic and spatial learning, tap students' musical intelligence by having them perform the song, *Clouds*.

Connections
Water vapor condenses into visible droplets when the moist, rising air cools to the dew point, forming clouds. Clouds influence temperature on Earth and also help us predict coming weather. And their myriad shapes paint the sky with beauty.

For the water cycle to continue, clouds must be present. Under the right conditions, the water or ice in some of them will fall to Earth. In the next group of activities, we will investigate precipitation.

Cloud Combos

How many cloud combinations can you make?

The three main types of clouds are cirrus, cumulus, and stratus. Other types of clouds are combinations of these clouds or use *nimbo* or *alto,* usually as a prefix.

Cut out the pictures at the bottom of the page. Try different combinations of two pictures to form new cloud words. List them below.

How would these clouds look? Where would they be in the sky?

Find pictures of these clouds. Draw a line through cloud names that meteorologists do not use. Why might they not be used?

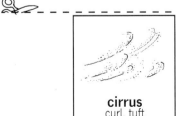

cirrus	cumulus	stratus	nimbus	alto
curl, tuft	heap, pile	stretched out, layers, sheets	rain	high (middle level)

Cloud Combos

How many cloud combinations can you make?

B

The three main types of clouds are cirrus, cumulus, and stratus. Other types of clouds are combinations of these clouds or use *nimbo* or *alto,* usually as a prefix.

Write two-word combinations in the connecting spaces.

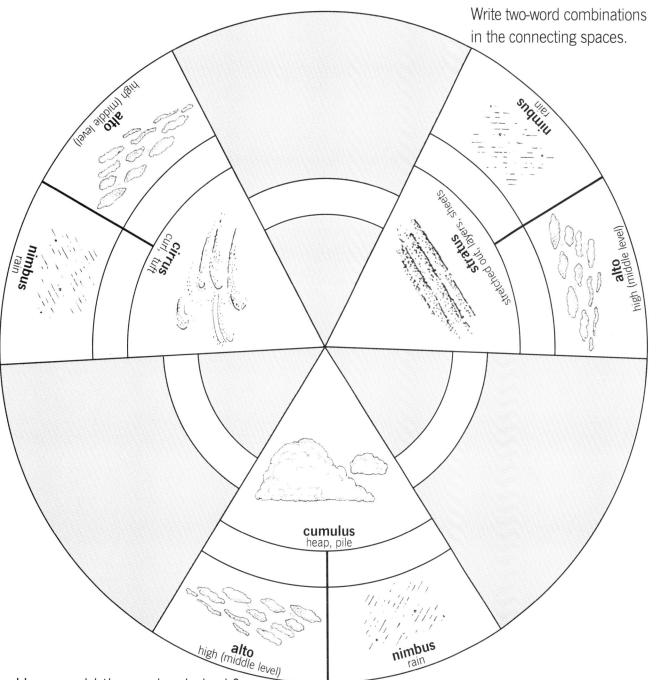

How would these clouds look?

Where would they be in the sky?

Find pictures of the combination clouds. Cross out the words and pictures that meteorologists do not use. Why might they not be used?

Cloud Combos

Cloud Table

Symbol	Cloud Type	Description	Composition	Height*	Related Weather	Forecast
	High					
	Cirrus (Ci)	wisps of hair, mare's tails, curls	ice crystals	above 6 km (20,000 ft)	fair	if warm front coming, can be first sign of storm (pattern: *cirrus to cirrostratus to altostratus to nimbostratus*)
	Cirrocumulus (Cc)	small bits of cotton, fish scales (mackerel sky)	ice crystals	above 6 km	fair	(see cirrus)
	Cirrostratus (Cs)	thin white sheet, halo around sun/moon	ice crystals	above 6 km	fair	
	Middle					
	Altocumulus (Ac)	rounded, shaded white/gray layers, often in rows	ice crystals or water droplets	2-6 km (6500-20,000 ft)	generally fair	summer thuderstorm if warm and humid
	Altostratus (As)	thicker, grayer, lower than cirrostratus, smooth sheet	ice crystals or water droplets	2-6 km	often covers entire sky, dims sun	may be followed by nimbostratus and stormy weather (see cirrus)
	Low					
	Nimbostratus (Ns)	darker than altostratus, dark sheet, can block sun	mostly water droplets	1-6 km	widespread, steady light-to-moderate rain or snow	
	Stratocumulus (Sc)	low gray or white patches, lumpy, cover most of sky	water droplets	below 2 km (6500 ft)	overcast	if follows storm, expect clearing skies; if darkens, expect rain/snow
	Stratus (St)	smooth, even layers, stretched out, blocks sun	water droplets	below 2 km	overcast; usually no precipitation; can be light mist, drizzle, snow grains; fog if low	
	Vertical					
	Cumulus (Cu)	heap or pile with flat base, detached, like cotton puffs	water droplets	1-5 km (3000-16,500 ft)	fair	if appears in moist, rising morning air, expect change to cumulonimbus and stormy weather; if appears in afternoon, exceect fair weather
	Cumulonimbus (Cb)	tall, billowing, white with dark base, top may be anvil-shaped	water droplets (lower), ice crystals (upper)	1-16+ km (3000-53,000+ ft)	thunderstorms—heavy rain, thunder, lightning; hail possible (cold front)	

* in temperate zones (Height will be lower at the Poles and higher in the Tropics.)

Cloud Combos

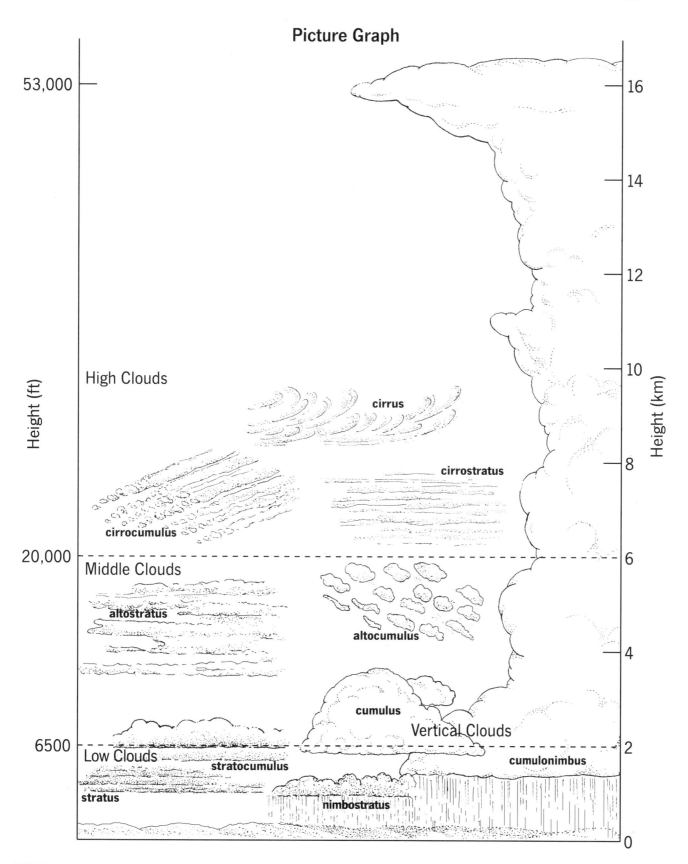

Picture Graph

High Clouds

cirrus

cirrostratus

cirrocumulus

20,000

Middle Clouds

altostratus

altocumulus

cumulus

Vertical Clouds

6500

Low Clouds

stratocumulus

cumulonimbus

stratus

nimbostratus

53,000

Height (ft)

16

14

12

10

8

6

4

2

0

Height (km)

Clouds

Words by Suzy Gazlay

Tune: Eency Weency Spider

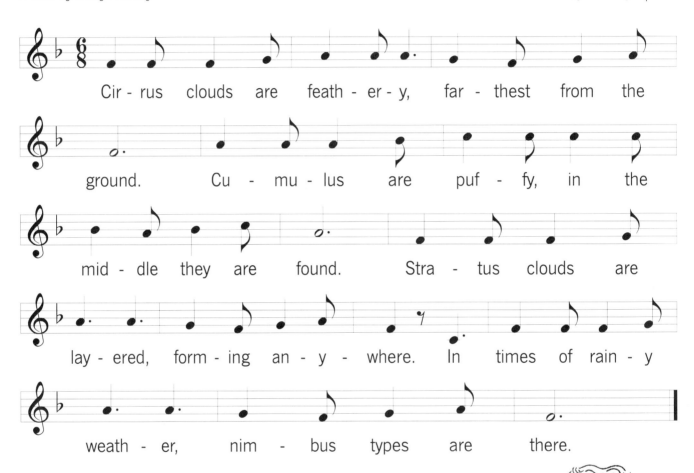

Cir - rus clouds are feath - er - y, far - thest from the
ground. Cu - mu - lus are puf - fy, in the
mid - dle they are found. Stra - tus clouds are
lay - ered, form - ing an - y - where. In times of rain - y
weath - er, nim - bus types are there.

Clouds

Cloud forms mix together,
    ten different types we see—
Cirrus, stratus, cumulus,
    the basic forms are three.
The rest are variations
    when two cloud types combine—
Puffy, dark, and wispy,
    or spread out in a line.

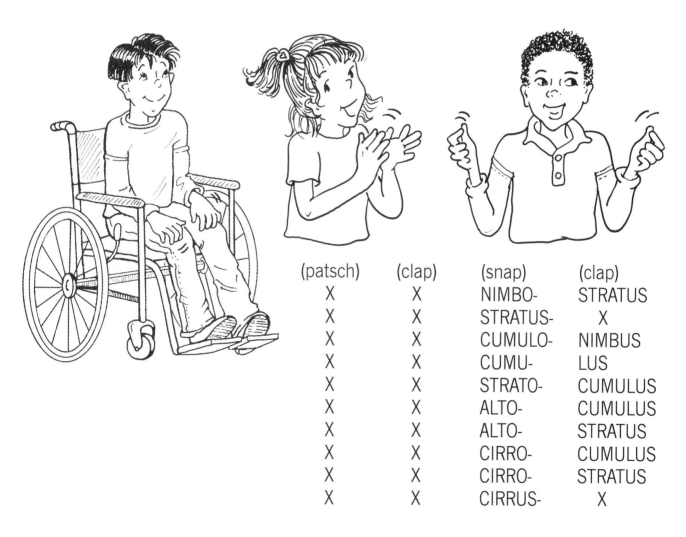

(patsch)	(clap)	(snap)	(clap)
X	X	NIMBO-	STRATUS
X	X	STRATUS-	X
X	X	CUMULO-	NIMBUS
X	X	CUMU-	LUS
X	X	STRATO-	CUMULUS
X	X	ALTO-	CUMULUS
X	X	ALTO-	STRATUS
X	X	CIRRO-	CUMULUS
X	X	CIRRO-	STRATUS
X	X	CIRRUS-	X

Fascinating Facts: Clouds

A typical cumulus cloud may weigh more than 400 metric tons, about the same as a fully-loaded 747. Cumulonimbus, huge thunderstorm clouds, may weigh several million tons.

Clouds contain less than 1 percent of all of the water—solid, liquid, or gas—circulating through the water cycle.

Sunlight bounces off the water and ice particles in clouds, scattering in all directions and making the cloud appear white. A very thick cloud will look dark because very little light can get through.

Condensation trails—contrails for short—are formed high in the atmosphere when water vapor from a jet condenses into ice crystals. The drier the air, the sooner the contrails disappear.

Rain Check

Topic
Weather station: precipitation
Concept of averaging: mean

Key Question
How can rainfall be measured?

Focus
Students will use a homemade rain gauge to measure rainfall. A real-world experience with averaging will aid in refining measurement estimates.

Guiding Documents
Project 2061 Benchmarks
• *When liquid water disappears, it turns into a gas (vapor) in the air and can reappear as a liquid when cooled, or as a solid if cooled below the freezing point of water. Clouds and fog are made of tiny droplets of water.*
• *Measurements are always likely to give slightly different numbers, even if what is being measured stays the same.*

NRC Standards
• *Weather changes from day to day and over the seasons. Weather can be described by measurable quantities, such as temperature, wind direction and speed, and precipitation.*
• *Water, which covers the majority of the earth's surface, circulates through the crust, oceans, and atmosphere in what is known as the "water cycle." Water evaporates from the earth's surface, rises and cools as it moves to higher elevations, condenses as rain or snow, and falls to the surface where it collects in lakes, oceans, soil, and in rocks underground.*

NCTM Standards 2000*
• *Select and apply appropriate standard units and tools to measure length, area, volume, weight, time, temperature, and the size of angles*
• *Understand the place-value structure of the base-ten number system and be able to represent and compare whole numbers and decimals*
• *Understand that measurements are approximations and understand how differences in units affect precision*
• *Use measures of center, focusing on the median, and understand what each does and does not indicate about the data set*

Math
Measurement
    length (depth)
Decimals
Averaging
    mean (division by twos and tens)

Science
Earth science
    meteorology
        water cycle

Integrated Processes
Observing
Identifying and controlling variables
Collecting and recording data
Comparing and contrasting
Interpreting data
Relating

Materials
Rain gauge containers, 2 per group (see *Management 1*)
Metric rulers or tenth-inch scales (see *Management 3*)
Wire or tape

Background Information
The Water Cycle and Rain
    The sun is the catalyst for the water cycle. As the sun heats the waters of the Earth, moisture enters the atmosphere (evaporation). The moist, warm air rises and cools. If it cools to the dew point, the water vapor condenses on tiny particles in the air, forming clouds. If enough moisture collects and grows to sufficient size, it returns to Earth as precipitation. The main forms of precipitation are rain, sleet, snow, and hail.
    Two theories, at present, explain the formation of raindrops. The *coalescence theory* applies to warm clouds, those composed of water droplets. These clouds are most often found in warmer regions of the world. As different-sized cloud droplets fall through the cloud at varying rates, they collide and combine. A million cloud droplets may merge to form one raindrop. When the droplets become large enough to overcome the buoyancy of the air, they fall to Earth as rain.
    Much of the world's precipitation, particularly in the temperate regions, develops in cold clouds, those composed of water droplets and at least some ice crystals. According to the *ice-crystal theory* suggested

by scientists in the 1930s, when ice crystals and water droplets are mixed together, the ice crystals will grow at the expense of the water droplets. In other words, the water droplets will attach themselves to the ice crystals. When the crystals become large enough, they descend toward Earth. If they reach warmer air in the lower atmosphere, they melt and become raindrops. The raindrops may continue to grow through coalescence as they fall to Earth (also see *The Water Cycle*).

Meteorologists define rain as droplets equal or greater than 0.5 mm in diameter. Droplets less than 0.5 mm are labeled drizzle.

Rainfall varies, influenced by the Earth's natural geography as well as features designed by people. The amount of rainfall a particular location receives is dependent on latitude, proximity to large bodies of water, land features such as mountains and valleys, air currents, and even the concentration of buildings and the degree of vehicle emissions in cities.

Rain Gauge

Rain gauges have been used since at least 1442 in the Korean Empire. Sir Christopher Wren, an English architect, introduced the first recording rain gauge in 1662.

Since 1870, the stick gauge has been the standard instrument used by meteorologists in the United States to measure rainfall and snowfall. It has a brass collector ring or opening eight inches in diameter. Raindrops that strike the sharp rim of the collector ring split, keeping the whole drop from sliding into the container and skewing the results. The collector ring is joined to a copper funnel with a $\frac{5}{8}$" opening (to help prevent water evaporation) and empties into a 20-inch long narrow tube where the rain is measured. Since the area of the tube's cross section is one-tenth that of the collector ring, one inch of rain will be 10 inches deep in this tube, making precise measurements to the nearest hundreth of an inch possible. The larger can around the tube holds overflow water from heavy storms which is then measured in turn.

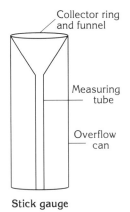

Collector ring and funnel

Measuring tube

Overflow can

Stick gauge

The homemade gauges in this activity will provide a more crude measure of rainfall but will give students a hands-on measuring experience and help them become aware of the variables involved. The size or shape of the container is not crucial, but it *is* crucial that the opening be the same size and shape as the rest of the container.

Management

1. A rain gauge must have straight or parallel walls, a flat base, and an opening the same diameter or width as the rest of the container. Measurements are easier to read if it is transparent.
   - For a permanent rain gauge, consider an olive jar, milk carton, tin can, coffee can, or graduated cylinder (cover the lip with tape.) To minimize evaporation in a round container, a funnel the same size as the opening may be attached, partially mimicking the container used by meteorologists.
   - For the averaging feature in this activity, multiple identical containers are required for the whole class. Milk cartons or tin cans are probably the simplest to obtain in quantity.
2. The rain gauge can be mounted on the top of a fence in an open area. Wire or tape can be used to place it in a level position and secure it against wind.
3. Meteorologists measure rainfall in millimeters or, in the U.S., hundredths of an inch. If using the tenth-inch scales, students will need to estimate hundredths. Copy the tenth-inch scales on transparency film and cut. Since copy machines distort slightly, adjust the machine so the copied scales match the inches on a classroom ruler.
4. Introduce this activity on a day when rain seems likely. Rain does not start or stop on cue, nor necessarily during school hours, so patience is warranted. Rainfall should be measured and poured out at your earliest convenience after a storm. The frequency of measurements will depend entirely on the weather patterns in your area.

Procedure

1. Read a few selections from *Rainy Day, Stories and Poems* (Caroline Feller, ed. HarperCollins. New York. 1986.) Encourage students to share experiences of when the rain was gentle and when it was pounding and fierce. Ask, "Which kind of rain is your favorite?" "Do you think all rains bring the same amount of water?" [No.] "How do you know?" [After heavy rains, there may be flooded roads and standing puddles that take a long time to disappear. After light rains, the sidewalks and driveways may dry quickly and water puddles disappear quickly.]
2. Explain that students will be setting up multiple stations to measure the rain. Distribute the activity page and read the directions together. Divide the class into five groups and distribute the rain gauge materials.

3. As a class, search for possible rain gauge sites outdoors. Have each group anchor their twin gauges in place.

4. After a rain, tell groups to measure and record the rainfall in each of their two containers. Ask, "How precise is your measurement?" (Examples: We had to guess a bit because it was hard to read the scale inside the milk carton. Our water line fell between two-tenths and three-tenths so we estimated it was 0.25 of an inch. Smaller units would help.)

5. To refine estimates, instruct each group to pour the collected water from one container into the second container. Have them measure again and divide by two to find the mean average. "How did the average compare to your original two measurements?"

6. To further refine estimates, have all the groups pour their collected water into one of the containers (or more if the rainfall were heavy). Together, take a water depth measurement and divide by ten (the number of containers used).
   • How does our class average compare to your previous measurements?
   • Why is the class average a better way to report our findings? [A lot of samples were combined, rather than just looking at one or two samples. We only measured once, instead of ten times, so there was less chance of human error. By calculating the average, we got a better idea of the hundredths place.]

7. Pour out the collected water and choose the gauge to be used for your weather station, perhaps something transparent. (See *Management 1.*) As precipitation occurs, add the measured depth to the station model (see the *Station Model* activity).

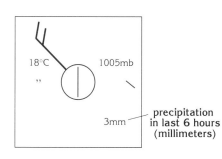

Discussion (Also see questions in *Procedure.*)
1. How would trees, buildings, or other structures affect the amount of water collected in a rain gauge? (Example: If the rain gauge were placed under a tree, the branches might prevent much of the rain from falling into the gauge.)
2. What are the advantages of the rain gauge containers we used? [meets the requirements of a rain gauge (parallel walls, flat base, opening the same size as the rest of container), easy to collect] ...the disadvantages? [not transparent, ruler has to be read at an angle, tin cans rust]

3. What kind of container would be best for our weather station? [probably a transparent one such as an olive jar or graduated cylinder unless following the procedure in *Extension 3]*
4. How much rain did this storm bring? (If the storm lasted more than one day and rainfall was measured at several intervals, measurements will need to be totaled.)
5. How do our measurements compare to official ones? If they are different, why do you think that is?
6. How did the barometer and wind change as the storm came through? [It is likely the air pressure lowered and the wind increased. (Also look at wind direction.)]

 Journal prompt: How does a rainy day make you feel? What do you like about it? What do you dislike about it?

Extensions
1. To prove that the shape or size of the container does not matter, as long as it meets the other requirements, have students collect rainfall in a variety of containers during one storm and measure depth.
2. Purposely place rain gauges at various places in the schoolyard to compare how rainfall totals may be affected by obstacles such as buildings and trees.

3. For a more precise measurement that reflects the method used by meteorologists, follow these instructions:
   - Collect a 2-lb coffee can and a small juice can. Mark the height of the juice can on the inside wall of the coffee can.
   - To find the volume ratio between the two cans, fill the smaller can with water and pour it into the larger can until the water reaches the marked height. The number of cans it takes gives a ratio, such as 9 to 1. Official rain gauges have a 10 to 1 ratio. The higher the ratio, the more precise the measurement.
   - Use the large can as the rain gauge. After it rains, pour the collected water into the small can. More than one small can may be needed. Measure the depth or combined depth and divide by the ratio. For example:

$$3.42" \div 9 = .38"$$
(estimated depth) (ratio) (rainfall)

4. Give students a map of the local area. Ask them to gather and record official rainfall data for neighboring towns from local broadcast stations, newspapers, weather radio, etc. "What, if any, rainfall patterns for our area did you observe?" (Examples: Rain does not fall evenly. There was more rain near the mountains. There was more rain in the north than in the south.)

Curriculum Correlation

Literature

Buchanan, Ken & Debby. *It Rained on the Desert Today.* Northland Publishing. Flagstaff, AZ. 1994. (The anticipation and wonder of a desert rain seen through the eyes of children. Beautiful watercolor illustrations. A "Reading Rainbow" book.)

Spier, Peter. *Rain.* Zephyr. Somerville, MA. 1987. (Two children enjoy the rain in this wordless book.)

Home Link

Students may wish to keep a rain gauge in their backyards.

Connections

The sun heats the Earth, driving the cycling of water from evaporation to condensation to precipitation. If enough moisture collects on the water droplets or ice crystals in clouds, they become heavy enough to fall to Earth. When the air temperature is above freezing, the precipitation will be in the form of rain.

We have measured rainfall on a day-to-day basis. This naturally leads to questions about larger rainfall patterns, over the month and the year. These will be explored in *Decimal Downpour.*

Rain Check

Constructing a rain gauge

Find a container with straight sides, a flat base, and an opening the same diameter or width as the rest of the container.

Place the container in an open area, away from buildings, trees, etc. Anchor it against winds. Make sure it is level and, preferably, off the ground.

After it has rained, use your ruler to estimate the depth of the collected water to the nearest millimeter or hundredth of an inch.

Date:

Time:

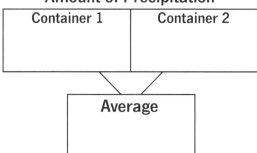

Amount of Precipitation

Container 1	Container 2

Average

Write the equation you used to find the class average.

Rain Check

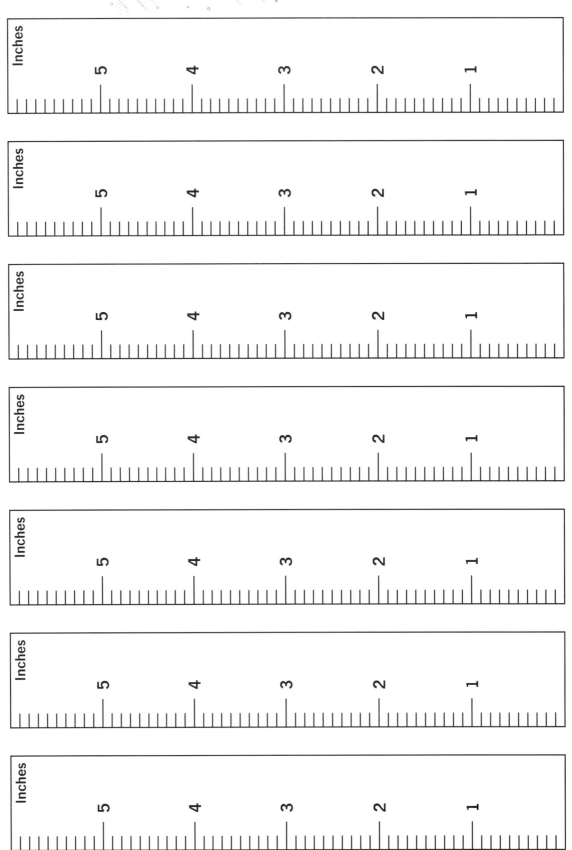

D.E.C.I.M.A.L Downpour

Topic
Annual precipitation

Key Questions
A: What are your rainfall patterns?
B: How does precipitation this year compare with precipitation over time?

Focus
Students will use the Internet to gather monthly precipitation data for their location, then graph and interpret the data. For *B*, students will compare normal precipitation with recent precipitation.

Guiding Documents
Project 2061 Benchmarks
- *When liquid water disappears, it turns into a gas (vapor) in the air and can reappear as a liquid when cooled, or as a solid if cooled below the freezing point of water. Clouds and fog are made of tiny droplets of water.*
- *Graphical display of numbers may make it possible to spot patterns that are not otherwise obvious, such as comparative size and trends.*
- *Things change in steady, repetitive, or irregular ways—or sometimes in more than one way at the same time. Often the best way to tell which kinds of change are happening is to make a table or graph of measurements.*
- *Use fractions and decimals, translating when necessary between decimals and commonly encountered fractions—halves, thirds, fourths, fifths, tenths, and hundredths (but not sixths, sevenths, etc.)*

NRC Standard
- *Weather changes from day to day and over the seasons. Weather can be described by measurable quantities, such as temperature, wind direction and speed, and precipitation.*

NCTM Standards 2000*
- *Understand the place-value structure of the base-ten number system and be able to represent and compare whole numbers and decimals*
- *Describe the shape and important features of a set of data and compare related data sets, with an emphasis on how the data are distributed*
- *Describe events as likely or unlikely and discuss the degree of likelihood using such words as* certain, equally likely, *and* impossible

Math
Decimals and place value
   rounding
   addition
Statistics and probability
Graphing
   bar, line
Measurement (optional)
   liquid volume

Science
Earth science
   meteorology
      water cycle

Technology
Gathering data on the Internet

Integrated Processes
Observing
Predicting
Collecting and recording data
Comparing and contrasting
Interpreting data
Relating

Materials
Internet connection (see *Management 1*)
Colored pencils
Fluorescent tube cover, optional (see *Management 4*)

Background Information
Rainfall varies with location and season. The amount of heat energy from the sun—directly related to *latitude*—drives evaporation. The proximity of large bodies of *water* makes it possible for substantial amounts of water vapor to enter the air. Because air is forced to rise (cooling and condensing) along their slopes, *mountains* often have significant precipitation on their windward side. The drier leeward region, sometimes a desert, is called the rainshadow.

Any form of water falling from the sky, whether liquid or frozen, is called precipitation. The precipitation measured by meteorologists includes anything that falls in the collection bucket, most often rain or snow. Depending on the type of weather station, the snow is either melted or weighed to determine the amount of water. Precipitation is reported in inches in the United States and in millimeters most everywhere else.

The water in melted snow does not necessarily equate with the *depth* of snow since wet snows and dry snows yield varying amounts of water. For this reason, meteorologists list snowfall depth separately.

Normals are defined as 30-year averages, generally three consecutive decades. They give a picture of weather over time, in other words, climate. The precipitation data for the most recent year may closely match the normal precipitation or it may differ greatly due to all the variables that affect atmospheric conditions and to extreme weather events like hurricanes.

The National Climatic Data Center (NCDC) computes updated normals from National Weather Service data every ten years. The current normals are for 1971-2000.

Based on the climatic data (normals), general probabilities such as likely or unlikely or equally likely can be stated. However, more specific probabilities tied to percents are not necessarily valid because the many variables affecting weather can cause wild swings in the current precipitation.

Management

1. Website with normal *and* recent precipitation data:
   http://www.wrh.noaa.gov/wrhq/nwspage.html
   (links to local National Weather Service websites)

   Websites with normal precipitation data:
   http://www.nws.mbay.net/normrain.html
   (NWS data for 300 U.S. cities in one table)

   http://www.usatoday.com/weather/waverage.htm
   (links to U.S./global weather averages)

   http://www.WorldClimate.com/
   (links to U.S./global normals)

2. Preview the chosen website. Organize a way to give smaller groups access to the Internet data or connect the computer to a larger screen, if available, so the class can gather data at the same time.

3. Choose one of the two options for doing this activity. *A* is easier; students round monthly precipitation for their location to the nearest tenth of an inch and complete a bar graph. The more challenging *B* requires students to gather both normal and recent precipitation data, round to the nearest tenth, and produce a line graph and a bar graph on the same grid for comparison purposes.

4. Optional: Obtain a 4-foot or 8-foot fluorescent tube cover from a hardware store. Seal one end with duct tape and have students pour water in it to illustrate the annual normal rainfall for your area.

5. Since precipitation is presently reported in inches in the United States, the table and graph are constructed for inches. If you want to use millimeters, please construct or have students construct the appropriate table and graph.

6. Cutting and gluing additional copies can extend the graph.

Procedure

A

1. Ask students to make these predictions:
   a. How much rainfall do you think our city receives in a year?
   b. In which month do you think we get the most rain?

2. Distribute the *A* page and have students write their location, prediction, and the data source.

3. Have students collect and record normal precipitation data from a website.

4. Help students round to tenths of an inch in the third column. If rounding decimals is not developmentally appropriate, give students the rounded numbers to record.

5. Direct students to complete the bar graph.

6. Study the data and look for patterns. Discuss the likelihood of getting rain in a particular month.

7. Have students fill a fluorescent tube cover with water, showing the total amount of rainfall received during a normal year.

B

1. Ask students to make these predictions:
   a. How much rainfall do you think our city receives in a year?
   b. In which month do you think we get the most rain?

2. Distribute the first *B* page and have students write their location, prediction, and the data source.

3. Have students collect and record normal precipitation data from a website. Also direct them to record the precipitation for the past 12 months or, if you prefer, for the most recent calendar year.

4. Suggest that students fold the data table in half lengthwise, so that only the normal precipitation columns are visible. Help students round to tenths of an inch. Flip the folded paper over and have them round recent precipitation.

5. Give students the graph page. Instruct them to use the light centerline within each bar to make a line graph of rounded normal precipitation. Make the line graph dark.

6. On the same graph, have students make a bar graph of the rounded recent precipitation.

Precipitation Key

——— Normal

░░░ Recent <u>2000</u>
(year)

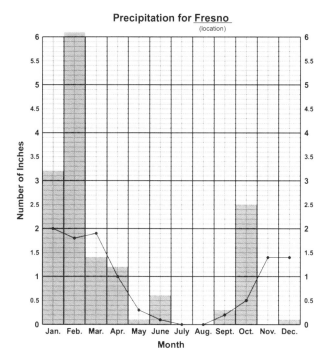

Precipitation for <u>Fresno</u>
(location)

Number of Inches (vertical axis)

Month (horizontal axis): Jan. Feb. Mar. Apr. May June July Aug. Sept. Oct. Nov. Dec.

7. Study the data, comparing the normal precipitation with the recent precipitation. Discuss the likelihood of getting rain in a particular month.

8. Have students fill a fluorescent tube cover with water, showing the total amount of rainfall received during a normal year. Empty the first tube or use a second tube to show the total rainfall for the last 12 months. (See illustration in *Procedure A-7.*)

Discussion

1. How would you describe our normal rainfall patterns?
2. Which months are the wettest? ...the driest? Do we have months in which it doesn't normally rain at all?
3. If there are unusual spikes in the data, what weather events caused all this rain? [hurricanes, tornadoes, etc.]
4. What is the likelihood of rain in _____ (name a month)? [impossible, unlikely, likely, certain] Explain.
5. What about our location encourages or discourages rain? (polar, temperate, or tropical region; abundance or lack of large water sources nearby; proximity to windward or leeward side of mountain range, etc.)
6. When a meteorologist says there is a 50% chance of rain, what does he or she mean? [It is equally likely that it will rain as it will not rain.] What if there is an 80% chance of rain? [It is very likely it will rain.] What if there is a 20% chance of rain? [Rain is not very likely.]
7. *B:* How does our recent precipitation compare to the normal precipitation?

Extension

Gather data for another location, preferably one that is much wetter or drier than yours. Compare the precipitation patterns of the two locations, using a United States map to reason how latitude or geographical features such as mountains might influence rain and snow.

* Reprinted with permission from *Principles and Standards for School Mathematics*, 2000 by the National Council of Teachers of Mathematics. All rights reserved.

Connections

The sun heats the Earth, putting the water cycle into motion. When enough moisture collects in the clouds, the droplets become heavy enough to fall to Earth. Unequal heating, the amount of available water, and other geographical features such as mountains are some of the variables determining how much precipitation a particular location will receive from month to month or year to year.

After examining long-term precipitation patterns, our attention now turns to a particularly interesting kind of precipitation—snow. Do all snowflakes have six points or sides? Discover the answer in *Families of Flakes.*

D.E.C.I.M.A.L
Downpour

Location: _____

Predicted annual precipitation: _____

Data source: _____

A

Precipitation (in)

Month	Normal	Rounded
January		
February		
March		
April		
May		
June		
July		
August		
September		
October		
November		
December		
Total		

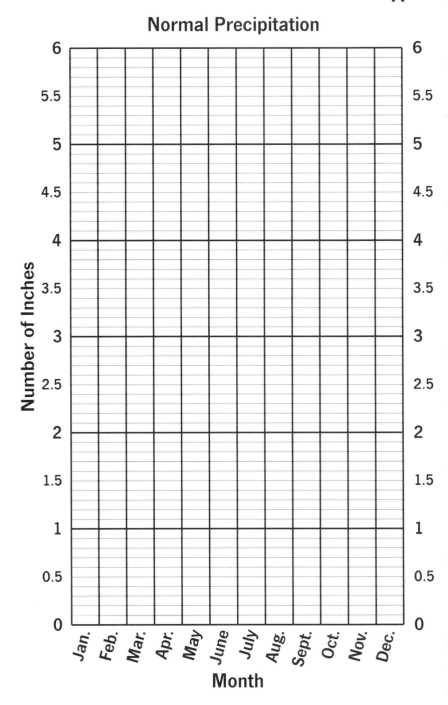

Normal Precipitation

Number of Inches

Month

D.E.C.I.M.A.L Downpour

How does precipitation this year compare with precipitation over time?

B

Location:

Predicted annual precipitation:

Data source:

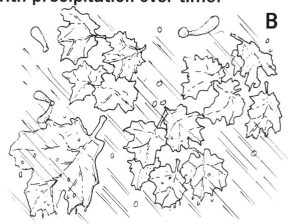

Month	Normal Precipitation (in)			Recent Precipitation (in)	
	Actual	Rounded		Actual	Rounded
January					
February					
March					
April					
May					
June					
July					
August					
September					
October					
November					
December					
Total					

D.E.C.I.M.A.L Downpour

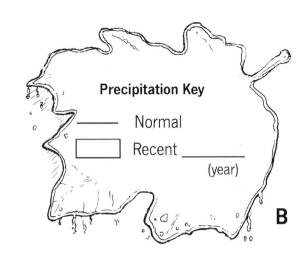

Precipitation Key

_____ Normal

[ ] Recent _____
              (year)

B

Make a line graph of the normal precipitation. On the same grid, make a bar graph showing recent precipitation. How do they compare?

Precipitation for _____
(location)

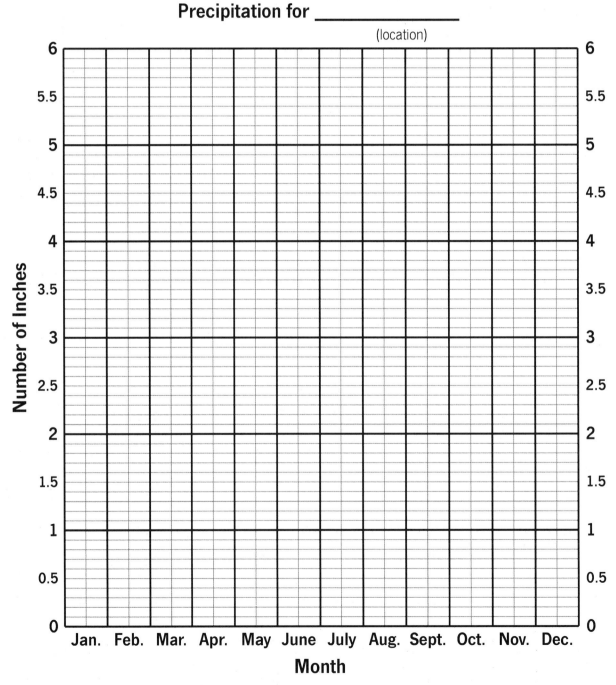

Number of Inches

Month

Raindrops are not shaped like teardrops. Most raindrops look like hamburger buns or hemispheres because, as they fall, the air pushing against them flattens their undersides.

The average raindrop falls at a maximum rate or terminal velocity of 6 m/s (20.5 ft/s). The larger the raindrops, the faster they fall.

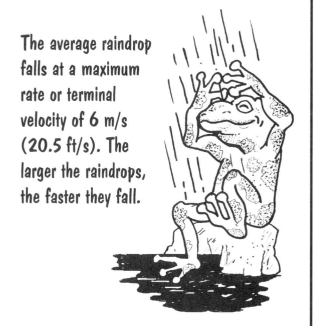

It's called rain if the droplets are greater than 0.5 mm in diameter and drizzle if they are smaller. The typical raindrop is 2 mm, 100 times larger than a typical cloud droplet. Beyond 5 mm, raindrops tend to split into several smaller drops.

Cloud droplet

Raindrop

In the U.S., rain is classified as ...
light (0.1 inch or less per hour)
moderate (.11 to .30 inches per hour)
heavy (>.30 inches per hour)

Each year, the Earth receives an average of about 86 cm (34 in) of precipitation, including rain, snow, sleet, and hail. In tropical regions, it may rain more than 1000 cm (400 in) a year while some desert areas receive practically no rain at all.

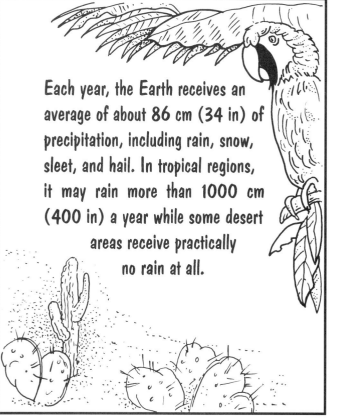

This activity begins a mini-unit on snowflakes. *Families of Flakes*, *It's Snowing!*, and *Snowflake Symmetry* are really three parts of the same activity, separated for clarity. *Families of Flakes* and *Snowflake Symmetry* can be explored regardless of climate. *It's Snowing!* requires falling snow. Normally an investigation would begin with real-world data but, in this case, a foundation of knowledge is first built in *Families of Flakes* so that students will be more astute observers when they examine real snowflakes in *It's Snowing!*

Families of Flakes

Topic
Classifying snowflakes

Key Question
How do snowflakes compare?

Focus
Students will group snowflake drawings by like characteristics and, in the process, discover that snowflakes come in a variety of shapes, some very unlike the "traditional" one with which they are probably acquainted. Their groupings will be compared to an international classification system used by meteorologists.

Guiding Documents
Project 2061 Benchmarks
• *When liquid water disappears, it turns into a gas (vapor) in the air and can reappear as a liquid when cooled, or as a solid if cooled below the freezing point of water. Clouds and fog are made of tiny droplets of water.*
• *Many objects can be described in terms of simple plane figures and solids. Shapes can be compared in terms of concepts such as parallel and perpendicular, congruence and similarity, and symmetry. Symmetry can be found by reflection, turns, or slides.*

NRC Standard
• *Water, which covers the majority of the earth's surface, circulates through the crust, oceans, and atmosphere in what is known as the "water cycle." Water evaporates from the earth's surface, rises and cools as it moves to higher elevations, condenses as rain or snow, and falls to the surface where it collects in lakes, oceans, soil, and in rocks underground.*

NCTM Standard 2000*
• *Identify, compare, and analyze attributes of two- and three-dimensional shapes and develop vocabulary to describe the attributes*

Math
Geometry and spatial sense

Science
Earth science
  meteorology
    water cycle

Integrated Processes
Observing
Comparing and contrasting
Classifying

Materials
Scratch paper (if cutting snowflakes in pre-assessment)
Scissors
Glue
12" x 18" light-colored construction paper

Background Information
Moisture in the air condenses, forming clouds. Clouds in the lower atmosphere are composed of water droplets. If a sufficient number of water droplets join together, they become heavy enough to overcome gravity and fall as rain. High clouds are made of ice particles. As more moisture condenses onto these ice or snow crystals, they too grow and fall toward Earth as snow. If they fall through air at freezing temperature (0°C or 32°F) or below, the precipitation will stay frozen, usually as snow. If they fall through air that is above freezing, the snow will turn to rain. If they fall through warmer air and then freezing air, the snowflakes will turn to rain and then refreeze as sleet. (See *The Water Cycle*.)

Snowflakes are composed of at least two, but often hundreds or thousands of crystals. The structure of the hydrogen and oxygen atoms in a water molecule causes them to bond with other water molecules at about 120° angles. For this reason, many snowflakes have a hexagonal appearance.

The beauty of snowflakes lies not only in their geometric patterns but also in their variety. The six-pointed snowflake most often represented in art is just one of seven types of snowflakes identified in the International Classification Chart for Solid Precipitation. The chart, in common use to this day, was devised in 1951 by the International Commission on Snow and Ice. In addition to seven types of snowflakes, it identifies three other types of solid precipitation: graupel, ice pellets, and hail. C. Magono and C. W. Lee developed another classification chart in 1966, one with over 70 categories!

The particular shape a snowflake has is determined foremost by temperature but also by the amount of moisture in the air, not only at the time of its birth, but also as it descends through the atmosphere. For example, needles form in a narrow temperature range, between -5°C and -8°C (23°F and 18°F). As snowflakes fall, their shape may change as more

118

moisture is collected or the temperature of the air becomes warmer or cooler. The strength of winds and angle at which snowflakes drift also influence shape. All these variables make it improbable that perfectly symmetrical crystals will reach Earth; in fact, they are relatively rare compared to the most common kind of snowflakes, irregular crystals which have no identifiable shape.

This activity has two purposes. First, it provides the preliminary knowledge needed to do field observations. If students think six-pointed snowflakes are the only real snowflakes, they are in danger of dismissing all the other snow crystal combinations as something other than snowflakes. Through exposure to other snowflake types, their view of snowflakes expands. This leads to the second purpose, a greater appreciation of the beauty and patterns to be found within nature.

Management
1. Cut the first activity page in half.
2. It is beneficial for each student to complete his or her own set of snowflake groups, but they are encouraged to discuss their choices within a small group of students.

Procedure
1. Distribute "What does a snowflake look like?" as a pre-assessment. Without giving any hints, have students draw or cut out what they think of as snowflakes.
2. In order to gain a sense of their present knowledge, encourage students to orally describe their examples. Save these papers to later compare with new learning.
3. Give students some background on how snow forms, then distribute "How are the snowflakes within each group alike?" as well as the two pages of snowflake drawings. Explain that these are all kinds of snowflakes. Instruct students to cut the snowflake boxes apart.
4. Invite students to study the snowflake drawings and group them by similar features.
5. Have students discuss their snowflake groups with two or three other students, asking them to describe what is alike about each group.
6. Distribute the *Solid Precipitation Chart*, explaining that this is one way meteorologists classify frozen or

solid precipitation. The first seven are snowflakes; the rest are other types of solid precipitation.
7. Have students study the chart, comparing the groups to the ones they have formed. Inform students that they may move any drawings so their snowflake groups match the ones on the chart.
8. Give each student a 12" x 18" sheet of light-colored construction paper on which to glue their snowflake families. Next to each group, direct them to write words describing how the snowflakes in that group are alike.
9. Referring back to the two half-sheets, have students compare their thinking at the beginning of the activity with their new knowledge.

Discussion
1. How difficult was it to group the snowflake drawings?
2. How do your groups compare with the *Solid Precipitation Chart*? (They were probably quite similar because the shapes are distinctive. Some students may have been puzzled about where to place the plates with arms, perhaps putting them with the plates, or the stellars, or making a separate group. That is perfectly all right as long as they can explain their reasoning. These particular shapes are sometimes called sector plates. When students eventually align their groups with those on the chart, however, the sector plates belong with the plates.)

Plate

3. How are snowflakes alike? How are they different?
4. What new things did you learn about snowflakes? [That the six-pointed stars are just one of several different snowflake shapes.]
5. From where does snow come? [It forms around ice particles in high clouds. If the air is freezing or below as it falls to Earth, we have snow.]

 Journal prompt: Describe your favorite personal snow adventure/experience.

Curriculum Correlation
See *Weather Literature* at the end of this book.

Connections
Snow forms in clouds where the temperatures are at or below freezing. If the air through which it falls is also at or below freezing, it remains as snow. The varied forms of these flakes are dependent on the coldness, moisture, and turbulence of the air.

Observations of snowflake families will now be applied to real snow in *It's Snowing!*, that is, if the weather in your location cooperates. If you live where it doesn't snow, a relative or friend who does may be willing to preserve samples for you.

Families of Flakes

What does a snowflake look like?

Draw or cut and glue some snowflakes here.

Families of Flakes

1. Cut out the snowflake drawings and put them in groups.

2. Compare your groups to those used by meteorologists.

3. Make any changes needed, then glue the snowflake groups on a piece of construction paper. Write describing words by each group.

How are the snowflakes within each group alike?

What new things did you learn about snowflakes?

Families of Flakes

All of these are snowflakes. How would you group them?

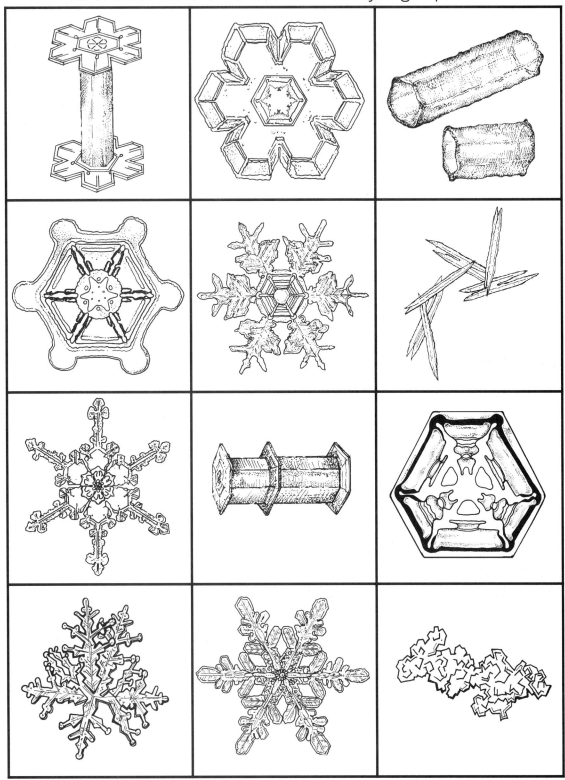

Most of these drawings were done directly from photographs in the book *Snow Crystals* by W. A. Bentley and W. J. Humphreys (Dover Publications, Inc. New York. 1962).

Families of Flakes

All of these are snowflakes. How would you group them?

Most of these drawings were done directly from photographs in the book *Snow Crystals* by W. A. Bentley and W. J. Humphreys (Dover Publications, Inc. New York. 1962).

Families of Flakes
Solid Precipitation Chart*

Example	Type	Symbol
	Plate	
	Stellar	
	Column	
	Needle	
	Spatial Dendrite	
	Capped Column	
	Irregular Crystal	
	Graupel	
	Sleet	
	Hail	

*classification by the International Commission on Snow and Ice
(The first seven groups are considered snowflakes.)

It's Snowing!

Topic
Snowflake observation

Key Question
How do the snowflakes compare?

Focus
Students will compare the characteristics of freshly-fallen and/or preserved snowflakes.

Guiding Documents
Project 2061 Benchmark
• *When liquid water disappears, it turns into a gas (vapor) in the air and can reappear as a liquid when cooled, or as a solid if cooled below the freezing point of water. Clouds and fog are made of tiny droplets of water.*

NRC Standards
• *Simple instruments, such as magnifiers, thermometers, and rulers, provide more information than scientists obtain using only their senses.*
• *Water, which covers the majority of the earth's surface, circulates through the crust, oceans, and atmosphere in what is known as the "water cycle." Water evaporates from the earth's surface, rises and cools as it moves to higher elevations, condenses as rain or snow, and falls to the surface where it collects in lakes, oceans, soil, and in rocks underground.*

NCTM Standards 2000*
• *Recognize geometric shapes and structures in the environment and specify their location*
• *Identify, compare, and analyze attributes of two- and three-dimensional shapes and develop vocabulary to describe the attributes*

Math
Geometry and spatial sense

Science
Earth science
    meteorology
        water cycle

Integrated Processes
Observing
Collecting and recording data
Comparing and contrasting

Materials
For the class:
    Snowflake Bentley by Jacqueline Briggs Martin
    1 thermometer to register air temperature

For fresh snowflakes, depending on options chosen:
    dark cloth, about 30 cm wide
    hand lens
    small paint brushes
    microscope slides or petri dishes (see *Management 1*)
    microscopes (see *Management 2*)

For preserving snowflakes:
    microscope slides
    clear acrylic spray such as Krylon®
    clothespins
    shoe boxes or other boxes with lids (see *Management 3*)
    microscopes

Background Information
Formation of Snowflakes
    A snowflake is not a frozen raindrop. It starts as a single ice crystal, formed only in clouds at or below 0°C (32°F). When the air cools to the dew point, the temperature at which it is saturated with water, the water vapor in the air most often condenses directly into ice around minute particles such as dust or salt spray. Sometimes, in the absence of the right kind of particles, the water vapor condenses as supercooled water, water that remains liquid below 0°C (32°F). The temperature may reach as low as -40°C (-40°F) before the supercooled water turns into an ice crystal.
    Vapor and supercooled water molecules collect and freeze on these ice or snow crystals, causing them to grow outward. Because of the way water molecules bond with each other, most snow crystals are hexagonal or six-sided. This six-sidedness is recognizable particularly when observing plates, stellars (also called planar dendrites), columns, and capped columns (see *Families of Flakes*).

124

Though not obvious with needles, spatial dendrites, and irregular crystals, these too have hexagonal patterns at the molecular level.

When the snowflakes become heavy enough, they begin to fall to Earth. Snowflakes change many times on their downward journey. Through collisions with other crystals, more crystals may become attached or break off. If snowflakes drift in gentle winds and parallel to the ground, condensed water vapor will be distributed evenly and the snowflake will be symmetrical, a relatively rare occurrence. Usually snowflakes fall in a lopsided manner, with water vapor condensing on some edges and not others. This is why the most common kind of snowflake is composed of irregular crystals with no recognizable form. Sometimes snowflakes, like capped columns, are a combination of more than one form. This happens as they pass through different temperature layers on the way down or while being carried higher in updrafts. By the time they reach Earth, multiple crystals—maybe two or maybe hundreds—will have joined together to make just one snowflake.

Snowflakes continue to change after they have landed, metamorphosing from light, airy crystals that form a natural insulation to settled, dense snow made of small, round grains. If change continues long enough, glacial ice can form.

No Two Alike?

Each snowflake follows a unique path as it descends to Earth. The temperature at which it was formed, the number of water molecules that became attached during its journey, the temperature of the various layers of air through which it traveled, among other variables, all determine its shape when it reaches Earth. For this reason, it is extremely unlikely that any two snowflakes are identical; the possible variations are too innumerable to calculate.

The primary variable is temperature, although moisture is a contributing factor.[1] Plates and stellars, for example, tend to form around -15°C (5°F) while needles form between -5°C and -8°C (18°F and 23°F). Dry snows have small, simple, harder crystals formed in low temperatures with low humidity. Wet snows are the result of higher temperatures—just below freezing—and higher humidity. Snowflakes passing through above-freezing air may melt and refreeze into pellets. Pellets that collect a coating of ice crystals become graupel.

According to the International Classification Chart for Solid Precipitation[2], there are seven families of snowflakes and three other kinds of frozen precipitation: graupel, ice pellets, and hail. This chart is applicable to falling snow only, not metamorphosed snow which has been laying on the ground for hours, days, or weeks.[3] Though not commonly used, Magono and Lee have since devised a more detailed classification system with over 70 categories!

Big Ideas

Observing snowflakes is a sensory experience; while the cold is nipping at your nose, you peer through the microscope at the most incredible shapes that have fallen from the sky. More than anything, this experience should inspire a sense of awe, a sense of the beautiful patterns in nature. Secondly, snowflakes are more varied than the hexagonal plates and six-pointed forms that are usually represented. All of the specimens that adhered to the slide are snowflakes, snow in forms which students may not have previously been familiar.

1. Temperature and moisture studies most often cited are those done by Ukichiro Nakaya (*Snow Crystals: Natural and Artificial*, Harvard University Press, Cambridge, MA. 1954) and C. Magono and C. W. Lee ("Meteorological Classification of Natural Snow Crystals," *Journal of the Faculty of Science, Hokkaido University*. November, 1966).
2. International Commission on Ice and Snow, 1951.
3. LaChapelle, Edward R. *Field Guide to Snow Crystals*. University of Washington Press. Seattle. 1969.

Management

1. For the slides and petri dishes, a glass surface seems to be friendlier to snowflakes than plastic but either may be used.
2. A microscope is the ideal tool for observing the intricate details of snowflakes. A magnification of 20x is recommended. Microscopes used to observe fresh snow should be able to tolerate cold and moist conditions. The Brock Magiscope®, available from AIMS, meets these criteria; it is also sturdy and draws light well. Reduce exposure to cold temperatures and moisture by putting the microscopes on a table in a sheltered area or, if out in the open, keeping them covered until needed. While using a microscope, brush away snowflakes as they accumulate.
3. Slides, acrylic spray, and any other materials that will be in direct contact with the snowflake samples should be kept at freezing temperatures for at least one hour before using. To prepare these materials, place them in a box, such as a shoebox or plastic toolbox, cover, and put in the freezer or leave outdoors in freezing weather. The slides used for preservation should be returned to this box and kept in freezing conditions until the spray is dry, an hour or more.

4. This activity is at the mercy of nature. Snow needs to fall during school hours and the colder the air temperature, the better. An air temperature of -4°C (about 25°F) or lower is recommended. At 0°C (32°F), the flakes usually melt before being preserved or observed. Wind should be minimal.

5. Students should bundle up in their coats, mittens, hats, and scarves to go outdoors. Allow students to step inside to warm up as needed. While collecting and viewing fresh snowflakes, a quick 10 or 15 minutes of observation is all that is needed.

6. Consider repeating these observations under different air temperature and moisture conditions (dry snow versus wet snow, morning versus afternoon).

7. Specimens for both fresh and preserved snowflakes may be captured at the same time. Study the options for viewing fresh snowflakes on the activity page and gather materials for those you want to try. Preserved snowflakes can be viewed whenever convenient and for as long as desired.

8. For those who do not live in snow country, try to persuade a relative or friend who does to preserve and send snowflake samples to you.

Procedure

1. Introduce the class to Wilson Bentley by reading the 1998 Caldecott Award-winning book, *Snowflake Bentley,* by Jacqueline Briggs Martin (Houghton Mifflin, Boston, 1998).

2. Distribute the *Fresh Snowflakes* page and review what students will be doing.

3. Go outside and give students any necessary materials that have been stored in freezing temperatures. Check the air temperature with a thermometer.

4. Encourage students to examine snowflakes and relate what they see to the snowflake families they studied in *Families of Flakes.* Urge them to watch the snowflakes as they melt too. As one teacher wrote, "...observing the melting was just as fascinating as the snowflakes. The dendrite [stellar] branches melt first but, as they melt, they appear to make little jumping movements. Each little jump moves the snowflake closer to the shape of a circle."

5. Back inside, have students respond to the two questions on the page and share their observations.

6. Give students the *Preserved Snowflakes* page or simply review what will be done.

7. Follow the directions for preserving snowflakes.

8. Have students observe the snowflakes imprints through microscopes, recording the types they see and any interesting features.

9. Save the preserved snowflakes for future use.

Discussion

1. How are snowflakes alike? [They are solids made of snow crystals. Many have six sides or six arms.]

2. How are snowflakes different? [Examples: Some, like the plates, have no holes. Others, like the stellars, are feathery and have arms sticking out. Others, like the columns, look like six-sided rods (hexagonal prisms). Some, like spatial dentrites, poke up into the air (three-dimensional). Some, like the irregular crystals, don't have any recognizable shape; they are like globs of ice.]

3. What kinds of snowflakes did you see? Which kind was most common?

4. How do the sizes of snowflakes compare?

5. What did you notice as the snowflakes melted? [melting began at the outer edges and moved toward the center, etc.]

6. What did you like about this experience?

7. After multiple snowflake observations: How do the snowflakes in a dry snow compare to those in a wet snow? How do the snowflakes in the morning compare with those in the afternoon? How do the snowflakes at the beginning of the storm compare to those later in the storm?

 Journal prompt: Use your five senses to describe snow. It may be helpful to make a list of adjectives first.

Connections

A snowflake's form when it reaches Earth is primarily dependent on the temperature of the layers of air through which it fell. The results have been directly observed as students applied their knowledge of snowflake families to actual snow. Next they will move back indoors to examine some geometric properties in *Snowflake Symmetry.*

It's Snowing!

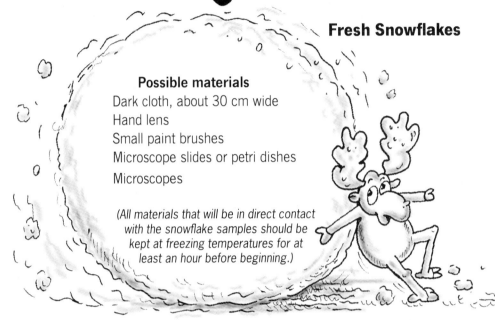

Fresh Snowflakes

Possible materials
Dark cloth, about 30 cm wide
Hand lens
Small paint brushes
Microscope slides or petri dishes
Microscopes

(All materials that will be in direct contact with the snowflake samples should be kept at freezing temperatures for at least an hour before beginning.)

- Collect some falling snow on a piece of dark cloth. Take the sample under an eave, tree, or other sheltered area so additional snow will not fall on it. Examine the shapes with a hand lens.

- A hand lens may also be used to examine the flakes that fall on your mittens or sleeves. You might even try to carefully brush or lift some onto a slide to look at under a microscope.

- Hold a cold petri dish out to catch falling snow. Take the sample to a moisture-tolerant microscope set up on a table outside and observe. When finished, tap the snowflakes out of the dish and gather some more.

- Use a small paint brush to lightly brush bits of snow from leaves, the edges of windows, or other surfaces onto a microscope slide or a petri dish. Aim for a small sample of fresh snow. Inspect the snowflakes.

Back inside...

What snowflake patterns did you see?

What did you notice as the snowflakes melted?

It's Snowing!

Preserved Snowflakes

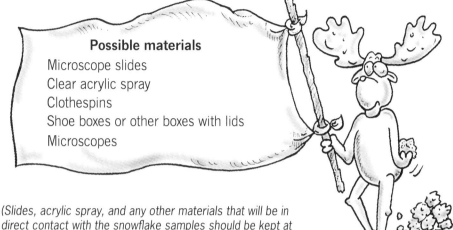

Possible materials
Microscope slides
Clear acrylic spray
Clothespins
Shoe boxes or other boxes with lids
Microscopes

(Slides, acrylic spray, and any other materials that will be in direct contact with the snowflake samples should be kept at freezing temperatures for at least one hour before beginning.)

1. Choose a time when snow is falling and the air temperature is below freezing; the colder, the better. An air temperature of -4°C (about 25°F) or lower is recommended. At 0°C (32°F), the flakes usually melt before being preserved.

2. Since body heat will warm the slide, hold a clothespin attached to one end of the slide.

3. In a sheltered area outdoors, hold the slide away from you and spray with a light coat of acrylic. Allow any excess to drip off a corner or turn the slide upside down for a few seconds to let the liquid settle.

4. Give the slide to a student and have him or her hold it in the falling snow for a few seconds. Students should not touch the slide or the acrylic spray.

5. Put the slide in a box, cover the box, and let it sit outside until dry, an hour or more. Although the snowflake itself will melt, an imprint of it will be left in the hardened acrylic spray.

6. Observe the preserved snowflakes through a microscope.

What snowflake patterns do you see?

Snowflake Symmetry

Topic
Line and rotational symmetry

Key Question
How does the symmetry of different types of snowflakes compare?

Focus
Students will explore the symmetry of two-dimensional drawings of several types of snowflakes.

Guiding Documents
Project 2061 Benchmark
- *Many objects can be described in terms of simple plane figures and solids. Shapes can be compared in terms of concepts such as parallel and perpendicular, congruence and similarity, and symmetry. Symmetry can be found by reflection, turns, or slides.*

NCTM Standards 2000*
- *Identify and describe line and rotational symmetry in two- and three-dimensional shapes and designs*
- *Recognize and apply mathematics in contexts outside of mathematics*
- *Use representations to model and interpret physical, social, and mathematical phenomena*

Math
Measurement
    angle
Geometry and spatial sense
    shape
    dimension
    symmetry

Science
Earth science
    meteorology
        water cycle

Integrated Processes
Observing
Collecting and recording data
Comparing and contrasting

Materials
For the class:
    1 transparent square (see *Management 1*)
    360° transparent protractor (see *Management 1*)

For each student:
    mirror or a piece of reflective material
      (see *Management 2*)
    pencil, tack/cardboard, or paper fastener
      (see *Management 3*)
    scissors

Background Information
Snowflakes
    The familiar star with six branches, called a stellar or sometimes a planar dendrite, is just one of seven different groups of snowflakes. Which shape will form is primarily determined by temperature variations, ranging from freezing (0°C or 32°F) on down. For example, needles form in comparatively warmer temperatures than stellars. By the time snowflakes reach Earth, many have lost their symmetry due to collisions, lop-sided drifting which causes moisture to be added unevenly, and temperature changes encountered on their journeys. In fact, the most common kind of snowflake is the irregular crystal.

    That snowflakes have symmetry at all is because of the way in which the hydrogen atoms in water molecules bond to each other. Sometimes this hexagonal structure can only be seen at the molecular level and other times it is visible in the multiple crystals of a particular snowflake. When water is frozen, this bond becomes more rigid. Those snowflakes that arrive on Earth with their symmetry intact indeed represent the incredible beauty of nature.

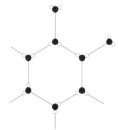

The hydrogen atoms are stuck to larger oxygen atom in an arrangement reminiscent of Mickey Mouse's head.

Symmetry

A figure has line symmetry if at least one line divides it into halves that are mirror images. This line, by definition, must pass through the figure's center point.

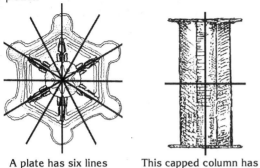

A plate has six lines of symmetry.

This capped column has two lines of symmetry.

A figure has rotational symmetry when its original image and orientation is repeated at least once as it is rotated 360° about a point. Although the number of repeated images can be counted, rotational symmetry is usually identified by the smallest possible angle measure between two repeated images. In the stellar snowflake below, the angle between the starting position and the first repeated image is 60° so we say the stellar has 60° rotational symmetry or its angle of rotation is 60°. This angle can also be found dividing the number of repeated images by 360°. For the stellar, the equation would be: 360° ÷ 6 = 60°

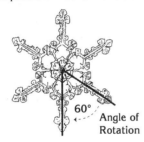

60° Angle of Rotation

Dimension

In this activity the line and rotational symmetry of two-dimensional drawings of snowflakes is being investigated. Real snowflakes are three-dimensional. Instead of line symmetry, they have plane symmetry. And the rotational symmetry is experienced differently. In two dimensions, a flat drawing remains in the same plane as it is turned around a point. In three dimensions, models are rotated or flipped in space. (See *Extensions.*)

Management

1. Using a transparency, draw or cut out a square. Label as illustrated, making one letter bold.

To model rotational symmetry, make a transparency of the 360° protractor found on the third student page. To facilitate discussion of observations, you may also wish to make a transparency of the four "rotational symmetry" snowflakes.

2. The reflective material needs to be 3" x 5" or larger and stiff enough to stay perpendicular to the fold line surface. Mirrors, colorful address card protectors (found in office supply stores), or colored acetate sheets cut to size meet these requirements. An additional choice is a Reflect/View, a colored sheet of Plexiglas with a built-in stand, available from AIMS.

3. Options for anchoring the center point about which a snowflake is rotated include pressing a pencil or finger against the point, pushing a tack through a double thickness of corrugated cardboard (about 2" x 2"), or attaching a paper fastener.

4. *Families of Flakes* is foundational to this exploration; *It's Snowing!* is desirable.

Procedure

1. Encourage the class to review some of their snowflake observations. Explain that they will be taking a closer look at the shape and repeating patterns within snowflakes in this activity.

2. Fold a piece of paper in half and cut out an irregular shape. Open the paper and display. Fold it again, explaining that one half matches the other half; they are reflections of each other.

   Open the paper again and position a mirror on the fold line, circulating so students can see. Tell them that the fold line is a line of symmetry, dividing the shape into two halves that are mirror images of each other. Explain that objects may have several lines of symmetry or none at all.

3. Give each student the *Line Symmetry* page and a mirror or other reflective material. Have them hold the mirrors perpendicular to the paper and through the center point to find and draw the lines of symmetry.

4. Discuss their observations.

5. Tell students that there is another kind of symmetry in which a figure is turned or rotated in one complete circle. If the starting image is repeated at least once during this 360° rotation, the figure has rotational symmetry. Put the transparent square and 360° protractor (see *Management 1)* on the overhead projector and rotate the square while the class counts the number of repeated images. [4]

Rotating Clockwise 360°

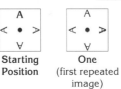

Starting Position

One (first repeated image)

Two

Three

Four

Return to the starting position, rotate, then stop when the figure repeats. Have students read the number of degrees rotated. [90°] Explain that we say this figure has 90° rotational symmetry or its angle of rotation is 90°. It could also be said it has four-fold symmetry because the figure is repeated four times during a 360° rotation.

6. Distribute the *Rotational Symmetry* page and snowflake drawings. Have students cut around the snowflakes, anchor the point of rotation (see *Management 3)*, and investigate the rotational symmetry from two different starting orientations.

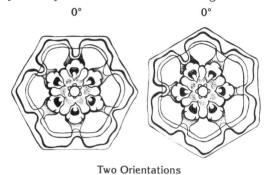

0°   0°

Two Orientations

Discussion

1. Which snowflakes have the same number of lines of symmetry? [plate and stellar—6; column and capped column—2; spatial dendrite—0]

2. Look at the International Snow Classification Chart from *Families of Flakes*. What might be said about the symmetry of needles? [Most often they are irregular, but it is possible for some to be evenly formed in which case they would have two lines of symmetry.] What might be said about the symmetry of irregular crystals? [They have no lines of symmetry.]

3. Which snowflakes have the same rotational symmetry? [plate and stellar—60° angle of rotation or six-fold symmetry; column and capped column—180° angle of rotation or two-fold symmetry]

4. If a plate is rotated around the protractor, at what positions does the image repeat? [60°, 120°, 180°, 240°, 300°, and 360°] What is the greatest common factor of these numbers? [60]

5. If the capped column has plates of two different sizes, what lines of symmetry would it have? [just one] What about its rotational symmetry? [It would have no rotational symmetry.]

6. Challenge: How are the number of lines of symmetry and the angle of rotation related? [The product of the two numbers will equal 360°. (For example, a column has two lines of symmetry and a 180° angle of rotation: 180° x 2 = 360°)]

7. What other objects in nature do you think would have similar symmetry? [The symmetry of honeycombs would relate to plates and stellars. The symmetry of some leaves would relate to columns and capped columns. (Pictures or actual samples would be helpful.)]

Extension

Have students study the plane and rotational symmetry of snowflakes in three dimensions by making paper models of columns, capped columns, and possibly spatial dendrites. See *Snowflake Artistry* for building techniques.

For plane symmetry, build a split capped column model. Show a plane of symmetry, akin to a line of symmetry in two dimensions, by placing a sheet of paper between the two halves of the capped column. Have students, using a card or piece of paper to represent the plane, visualize splitting their capped column models in half in as many ways as possible. If the capped column had a smaller plate on top than on the bottom, how would its plane symmetry differ?

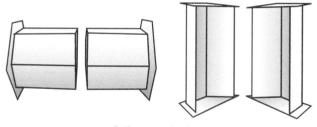

Split capped column

For rotational symmetry, have students manipulate their models in space. Identify a starting position and then turn or flip the model about a point so that it repeats the position and shape used in the beginning. How many different ways can this be done while making one complete circle? What different starting positions can be used?

Connections

The geometry of snowflakes is derived from the angle at which water molecules bond to each other. Appreciation for the beauty of the hexagonal patterns is enhanced by studied observations of their symmetry.

These glorious shapes of nature also play an important role in the water cycle. Snowflakes are a form of precipitation that, when melted, replenish the Earth with water. The water content of snow is the focus of the next activity, *Snow Job.*

Snowflake Symmetry

Line Symmetry

Place a mirror across the center of these two-dimensional snowflake drawings. In which positions do you see the whole snowflake, one half reflecting the other half? Draw all of these lines of symmetry. How many does each snowflake have?

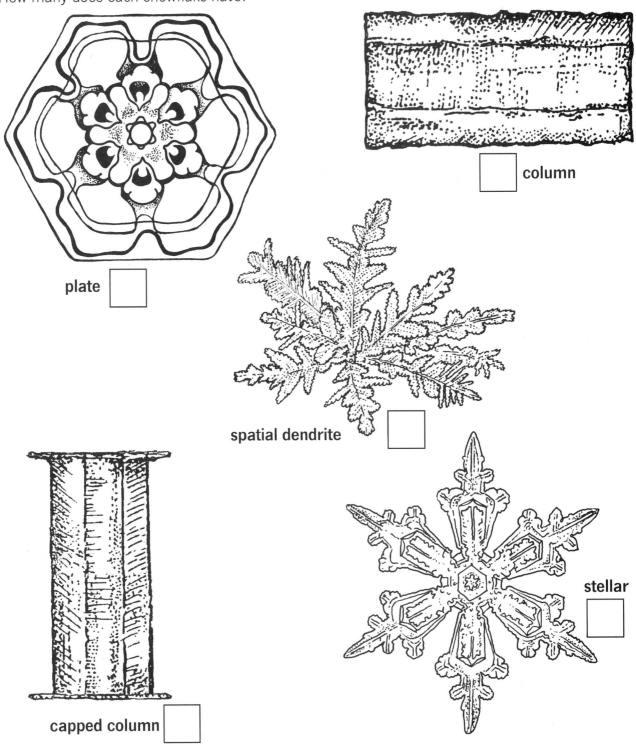

column

plate

spatial dendrite

capped column

stellar

Sn❄wflake Symmetry

Cut out these snowflakes to use on the rotational symmetry page.

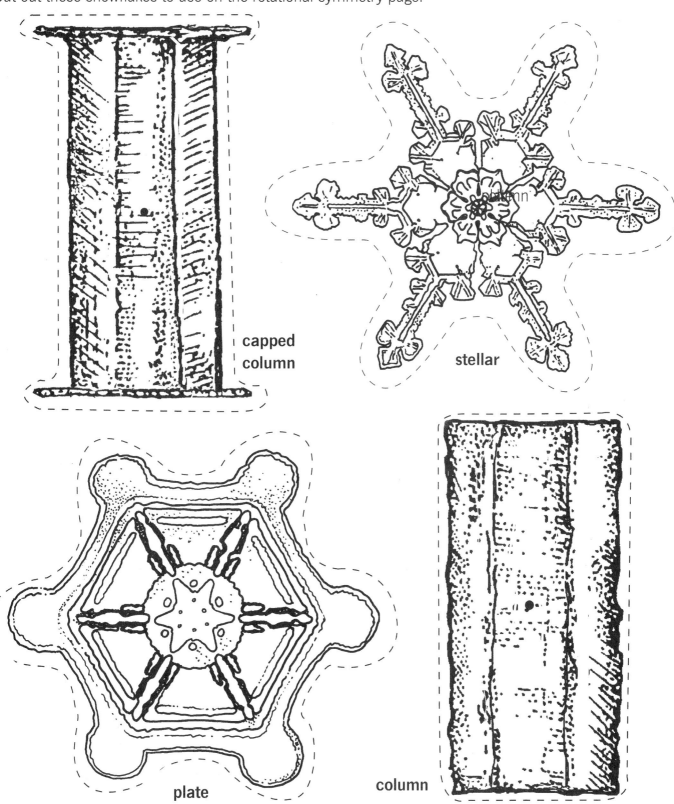

capped
column

stellar

plate

column

Sn❄wflake Symmetry

Rotational Symmetry

Center the snowflake drawings, one at a time, on the protractor. Rotate the snowflake in one complete circle, counting how many times the snowflake looks the same as it did in its starting position. Use the protractor to find the angle of rotation.

Count	Type of snowflake	Angle of rotation
	plate	
	stellar	
	column	
	capped column	

Snow Job

Topic
Water content of snow

Key Question
How much water is in your snow?

Focus
Students will compare the mass and volume of a snow sample before and after it melts.

Guiding Documents
Project 2061 Benchmarks
- *When liquid water disappears, it turns into a gas (vapor) in the air and can reappear as a liquid when cooled, or as a solid if cooled below the freezing point of water. Clouds and fog are made of tiny droplets of water.*
- *Make sketches to aid in explaining procedures or ideas.*
- *Use numerical data in describing and comparing objects and events.*

NRC Standards
- *Simple instruments, such as magnifiers, thermometers, and rulers, provide more information than scientists obtain using only their senses.*
- *Materials can exist in different states—solid, liquid, and gas. Some common materials, such as water, can be changed from one state to another by heating or cooling.*
- *Weather changes from day to day and over the seasons. Weather can be described by measurable quantities, such as temperature, wind direction and speed, and precipitation.*
- *Water, which covers the majority of the earth's surface, circulates through the crust, oceans, and atmosphere in what is known as the "water cycle." Water evaporates from the earth's surface, rises and cools as it moves to higher elevations, condenses as rain or snow, and falls to the surface where it collects in lakes, oceans, soil, and in rocks underground.*

NCTM Standards 2000*
- *Recognize and apply mathematics in contexts outside of mathematics*
- *Select and apply appropriate standard units and tools to measure length, area, volume, weight, time, temperature, and the size of angles*

Math
Measurement
    mass
    volume
Graphing, bar
Ratios and percents, optional

Science
Earth science
    meteorology
        water cycle

Integrated Processes
Observing
Predicting
Collecting and recording data
Comparing and contrasting
Generalizing

Materials
For the class:
    snow
    containers to collect snow (see *Management* 1)
    several pieces of cardboard (see *Management* 2)
    masking tape
    balances
    gram masses

For "Going Further":
    metric rulers and/or mL measurers (cups or graduated cylinders)
    calculators, optional

Background Information
Snow: Formation, Mass, and Volume

    Water, in its varied states, continuously cycles between the Earth and the atmosphere. Some of the water that evaporates into the air may eventually condense and appear as clouds. In clouds colder than 0°C (32°F), water vapor condenses directly into ice. Ice crystals fed by more moisture may become heavy enough to fall to Earth as snow, if the layers of air through which they fall are also below freezing. When the snow melts, it returns to a liquid state and the water cycle continues.

    As a given amount of snow changes from solid to liquid, its *mass* remains the same. This follows the law of conservation of matter.

However, the *volume* does change when fresh snow melts. Ten centimeters of fresh snow may yield as little as 0.1 cm (100 to 1 ratio) or as much as 4 cm (2.5 to 1 ratio) of water. That is a range of 1% to 40% water. The commonly mentioned ratio of 10 cm snow to 1 cm melted snow is a quick first guess and tends to be on the high end for snows in the United States; only measuring will give the actual results for a particular snow.

Whether a snow will be wet or dry depends primarily on the temperature in which it forms and falls. Wet snow develops at relatively warmer temperatures, freezing (0°C) or just below, because the air's capacity for moisture is greater and because this moisture can exist both in the form of ice crystals and liquid water (supercooled water droplets). The supercooled water attaches and fills the spaces within the crystal snowflake, increasing its liquid content. Dry snow develops in very cold air, usually -15°C or below, in which less moisture is present and in which there is less chance that supercooled water droplets exist.

If snow crystals have so little frozen water, what makes up the missing volume? Air. Fresh, uncompacted snow is generally 90-95% air! These pockets of air between and within snowflakes allow the snow to have insulating properties.

Measuring the Water Content of Snow

Meteorologists measure the water content of snow in two ways. Snow is collected in the same stick gauge used to collect rain. After the snow melts, the amount of water is measured. A core sample of snow may also be taken and weighed with the snow still in its frozen form. The mass remains the same, whether solid or liquid. One gram is equal to 1 milliliter.

Snow surveyors in California collect snowpack data in order to forecast the volume of seasonal river runoff. They use 30-inch tubes with a diameter of 1.5 inches. Several tubes may be joined together to measure a deep snow. The tube is driven into the snow until it reaches the ground underneath and the snow depth read on the tube's ruler-type scale. The tube is removed, snow core intact, and weighed. The snow core is then dumped out and the empty tube weighed. The water content is determined by subtracting the weight of the empty tube from the weight of the snow-filled tube.

Management

1. Collect identical containers with straight sides such as tin cans or jam jars.
2. Cardboard pieces, cut larger than the container opening, will be used to shave the snow even with the container's opening. Several students can share one piece.

3. Cut strips of masking tape about 2 cm long and 0.5 cm wide, one per student.
4. While waiting for the snow to melt, read a book about snow (see *Weather Literature)* or continue with other curriculum.

Procedure

1. Hold up a container and ask, "If this container is filled with snow, how much water will there be when it melts?" (Field guesses.) Explain that each student will test a sample of snow.
2. Distribute the first activity page and materials. Have students predict the water level by placing a thin strip of masking tape on their containers. Point out that they will be describing the snow and should observe it carefully while outdoors.
3. Make sure students dress warmly. Then take them outside and find some fresh, undisturbed snow, if possible.
4. Explain that it is important to gather a sample that preserves the snow in the condition it is found, without deliberately pressing or packing. "Turn your container upside down and push it gently into the snow until the snow touches the bottom of the container. Take the cardboard, push it across the container's opening, and turn your sample right-side up. Then let someone else use the cardboard."
5. Direct students to collect their snow samples, return indoors to measure the mass (container included), and write their snow descriptions.
6. After the snow has melted, have students measure the mass and make informal observations about the change in volume (less than one-half, etc.). Instruct them to draw their container showing predicted and actual water levels.
7. Guide a class discussion on their observations and conclusions.

Going Further...

1. Encourage students to quantify the change in volume, having them brainstorm ways this could be done.
   - *Method 1*: If the container has straight sides, a metric ruler can be used to measure the depth of the snow and, later, the depth of the melted snow.
   - *Method 2*: Fill the container with water and pour it into a mL measurer to find the volume of snow that it will hold. Measure the melted snow in the same way.

   For either method, calculate the percent of water in snow:

   (melted snow ÷ snow) x 100

2. Distribute the second page and have students describe and carry out their chosen method, complete with graph of measures or percents.

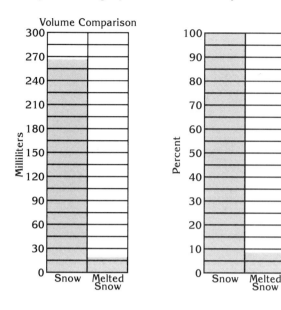

Volume Comparison

Discussion
1. How do the masses of snow before and after it melted compare? [They are the same.]
2. How do the volumes of snow before and after it melted compare? [There is very little water compared to the amount of snow, most likely less than 10% or one-tenth.]
3. What, besides water, makes snow fill more space? (Students might infer that it is air that makes up the difference.)

4. How is snow related to the water cycle? [It is a kind of precipitation. The melted snow feeds the rivers, soaks into the ground to replenish the water table, and some evaporates to continue the water cycle.]
5. What new question would you like to investigate? [Does snow always have the same amount of water? What conditions might make the snow wetter or drier?] Develop a plan to carry out your investigation.

Extensions
1. Repeat this activity after another snow and compare the results.
2. Have students devise an investigation to measure the water content of snow by weighing core samples. See the website listed in *Curriculum Correlation.*
3. How does the snow's temperature change as it melts in their container? Take the temperature of the snow at regular time intervals as it melts. Make a graph.
4. Measure the masses and volumes of ice before and after it melts. Compare the results to snow.

Curriculum Correlation
Technology
   To see pictures and a description of how snow surveys are taken in California, go to this website and access the menu item, "How a Survey is Made": http://cdec.water.ca.gov/snow/

Connections
   The temperature of the environment in which the snowflake develops determines whether snow will be wet or dry. The air's greater capacity for moisture at relatively warmer temperatures, at or just below 0°C, encourages the development of wet snow. So temperature not only affects whether the Earth receives rain, sleet, snow, or hail, but how much water the precipitation will yield.
   As precipitation melts and accumulates, the water cycle continues. The activity, *Water Go-Round,* can be used to assess whether students have related their observations within specific activities to the broader picture of the water cycle.
   An additional assessment on weather tools and scales, related to the combined experiences presented in the two volumes of *Weather Sense,* is also included.

Snow Job

How much water is in your snow?

Describe your snow sample, including its age and where you found it.

Mark the predicted melted snow level on your container. Draw your container showing the predicted and actual water levels.

Mass in grams

Snow	Melted Snow

What did you learn about mass?

What did you learn about volume?

Snow Job

Going further...

Using numbers, find a way to compare the volume of snow before and after it melts. Explain and record what you did. Show the data on the graph.

Challenge: Find a way to get more water from a container full of snow.

Snowflake Bentley

Wilson A. Bentley was fascinated with snowflakes. During winters on his hillside farm in Jericho, Vermont, he patiently caught snowflakes on a smooth black board about 30 cm square. After a moment or two, he would quickly duck into a sheltered area, inspect them with his magnifying glass, and transfer the ones he wanted to a glass slide. He used a small wing feather to gently press them flat. In his open-air woodshed outfitted with a photomicrograph camera—a microscope and camera joined together—Mr. Bentley captured nature's beauty for all of us to see. Starting in 1885 and continuing over the next 46 winters, he photographed over 5000 snowflakes, earning him the nickname, Snowflake Bentley. In 1931, many of these photographs were published in a book called *Snow Crystals* by W. A. Bentley and W. J. Humphreys.

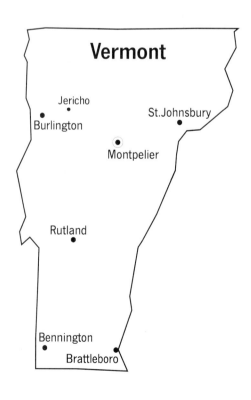

Vermont

Jericho
Burlington
St.Johnsbury
Montpelier
Rutland
Bennington
Brattleboro

Read *Snowflake Bentley,* the Caldecott-award winning book by Jacqueline Briggs Martin with illustrations by Mary Azarian (Houghton Mifflin, New York, 1998).

Snowflake Artistry

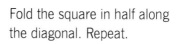

Fold the square in half along the diagonal. Repeat.

Paper Snowflakes

Use squares of scratch paper or recycled holiday wrapping paper to make six-sided paper snowflakes. An effective way to model folds is by using waxed paper on the overhead projector.

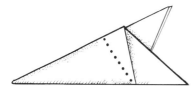

Fold into thirds, adjusting the folds until the edges meet.

Trim the open edge. Use decorative cuts to make a unique snowflake.

What kind of cuts would you need to make a plate?
How about a plate with sectors? How about a stellar snowflake?

Compass Snowflakes

1. Draw a circle with the compass. Without changing the compass arms, make a short line intersecting any point on the circle.
2. Put the compass point on the intersection. Swing the pencil arm until it touches another point on the circle. Draw a small intersecting arc.
3. Move the compass point to the new intersecting point. Repeat until you return to the first point.
4. Connect adjacent points using a ruler. Lightly draw the diagonals through the center of the circle and add symmetrical designs with colored pencils or by gluing on construction paper shapes.

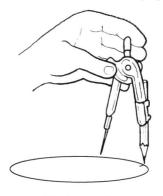

Circle marks

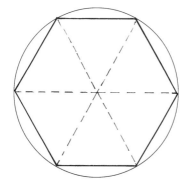

Lines

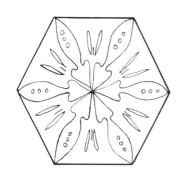

Snowflake design with six lines of symmetry

Snowflake Artistry

Pattern Block Snowflakes
Build outward from a hexagon to make a variety of plates and stellars.

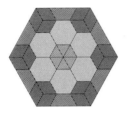

Plate

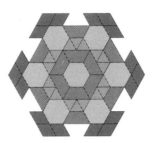

Plate with Sectors

Stellar

Snowflakes in Three Dimensions
Use paper to build columns, capped columns, needles, and spatial dendrites.

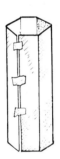

Column
Fold a rectangle into 6 sections and tape.

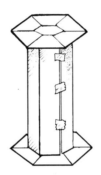

Capped Column
Add a plate or plate with sectors to each end of a column.

Spatial Dendrite
Make a free-form snowflake with feathery arms going in all directions.

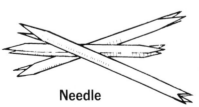

Needle
Roll paper to resemble toothpicks. Attach some together.

Make a display, possibly a mobile, of both two- and three-dimensional paper snowflakes.

Fascinating Facts: Snow

Snowflakes range in diameter from a dot on the letter i to several centimeters. Most snowflakes are less than one centimeter wide.

1 cm

Though the stellar snowflake may be most familiar, the most common kind of snowflakes are irregular crystals with no identifiable form.

The interior of Antarctica qualifies as a desert (<25 cm of precipitation annually). The cold, relatively dry air produces no rain and only a small amount of snow, equaling less than 5 cm (2 in) of water a year.

The Inuits (IN-oo-its) of the Kobuk (KO-book) Valley in northwest Alaska have many words for snow.*

annui	falling snow
api	snow on the ground
pukak	sugar snow, can cause avalanches (loose, hard, round crystals act like rolling ball bearings)
qali	snow that collects on tree branches
kanik	rime (frosty coating of ice found on tree trunks, some falling snowflakes, etc.)
upsik	hard, compact, wind-beaten snow
siqoq	swirling (fierce) or drifting (gentle) snow blown upward by the wind
kimoagruk	snow drift (siqoq piled up and at rest)
qamaniq	bowl-shaped hollow around the base of a tree (shallow snow)
siqoqtoaq	sun crust (wet and granular snow, called "corn snow" or spring slush by skiers)

Inuit vowel pronunciations

a = ah, as in saw
e = ey, as in prey
i = i, as in stick
o = o, as in bone
u = oo, as in tool

* Williams, Terry Tempest and Ted Major. The Secret Language of Snow. Sierra Club/Pantheon Books. San Francisco. 1984.

Moisture

Essential Question

How does water move from Earth to sky and back?

Learning Goals

• Observe and gather evidence that water endlessly cycles through evaporation (humidity), condensation (clouds and dew), and precipitation (rain and snow), causing a variety of weather conditions.

- Discover that water evaporates at different rates and results in humidity.
- Explore how water vapor condenses as frost or dew or as a variety of clouds that contribute to the unequal heating of the Earth.
- Investigate rainfall patterns and how precipitation, particularly rain and snow, replenishes the Earth with water.
- Appreciate the beauty of clouds and snowflakes and identify their forms.

Moisture Assessment

As students complete each water cycle activity in this book, they should reflect on how their learning relates back to the essential question: *How does water move from Earth to sky and back?* Specific knowledge needs to be connected to the bigger picture—how the processes are related, how they combine to make a whole.

Water Go-Round, the activity that follows, is intended as a culminating assessment experience. Students are asked to demonstrate how they have integrated the specific into the whole through observation of a water cycle model and the creation of a pictoral/written display. Procedural directions and a rubric to evaluate learning are included.

Topic
Water cycle assessment

Key Question
How does water move from Earth to sky and back?

Focus
Students will observe a water cycle model and then relate it and previous learning to the water cycle in nature.

Assessment Goals
- Follow directions for setting up the model.
- Observe and identify water cycle processes in the model.
- Illustrate and label the parts of the natural water cycle.
- Write one or more paragraphs explaining the water cycle. Include the weather conditions the cycle causes.

Guiding Documents
Project 2061 Benchmarks
- *When liquid water disappears, it turns into a gas (vapor) in the air and can reappear as a liquid when cooled, or as a solid if cooled below the freezing point of water. Clouds and fog are made of tiny droplets of water.*
- *Geometric figures, number sequences, graphs, diagrams, sketches, number lines, maps, and stories can be used to represent objects, events, and processes in the real world, although such representations can never be exact in every detail.*
- *Make sketches to aid in explaining procedures or ideas.*

NRC Standard
- *Water, which covers the majority of the earth's surface, circulates through the crust, oceans, and atmosphere in what is known as the "water cycle." Water evaporates from the earth's surface, rises and cools as it moves to higher elevations, condenses as rain or snow, and falls to the surface where it collects in lakes, oceans, soil, and in rocks underground.*

Science
Earth science
    meteorology
        water cycle

Integrated Processes
Observing
Predicting
Collecting and recording data
Comparing and contrasting
Relating

Materials (Choose one model.)
Outdoors model, per pair of students:
    9 oz. wide-mouthed transparent cup
    black construction paper or brown paper towels
    about 20 mL of water at room temperature
    1 ice cube
    hand lens, optional

Indoors model, per pair of students:
    9 oz. wide-mouthed transparent cup
    plastic wrap
    hot water
    1 ice cube
    hand lens, optional

Background Information
Water continually circulates between the Earth's surface, the air, and underground, changing form but not increasing or decreasing in total volume. About 97 percent of this water is the salty water found in the oceans. The other 3 percent is fresh water, most of it in glaciers and icecaps with smaller amounts underground, in rivers and lakes, and in the atmosphere.

The circulation of water is driven by heat energy from the sun. As the sun warms the surface of oceans and other water sources, the movement of water molecules quickens and some escape to become water vapor in the atmosphere. If cooled, the vapor molecules slow down and condense on tiny particles in the air and fall back to Earth as liquid or solid precipitation.

The water cycle contributes to a variety of weather conditions. Evaporation causes humidity that is sometimes uncomfortable if combined with warm temperatures. Condensation produces frost, dew, and clouds. Numerous, thick clouds can block much of the sun's radiation while thin or few clouds allow the heat energy to move freely, affecting temperatures on Earth. Gentle or more turbulent storms bring precipitation in the form of rain, sleet, snow, or hail.

Management

1. Choose the water cycle model to be used. For the outdoor model, a day with little cloud cover, low relative humidity, little wind, and temperatures in the mid 60s (°F) or higher is desirable.
2. On a surface large enough for the class to see, such as chart paper or the chalkboard, write the standards you will use for the assessment.
3. Place the materials on a table where student pairs can gather what they need.
4. If an extended time period is available, this activity can be done in one day. Or you may prefer to do *Part One* on one day and *Part Two* on the following day.

Procedure

1. Since this is an assessment, explain the standards you will use.
2. Give student pairs the activity page. Have them gather the needed materials for *Part One*, perform the investigation, and record their observations. Observations should last about 15 minutes.
3. Optional: Suggest students use permanent pens to draw features of the natural water cycle on the parts of the cup where those processes take place.
4. Distribute the chart paper and have student pairs illustrate and write about the natural water cycle as instructed in *Part Two* on the activity page.
5. The collection of papers may be followed by *Discussion*.

Discussion

1. How is the water cycle model like the water cycle in nature? [It shows accumulated water, condensation, and maybe precipitation. Evaporation can be inferred though not directly seen.]
2. How is the model different from nature? [Both models are comparably tiny and shielded from some of the variables interacting in the vast arena of Earth and its atmosphere. The *indoors model* does not have an outside or external heat source such as the sun. Precipitation may not have taken place in the *outdoors model,* possibly due to lack of water or the short observation time.]
3. What processes are easy or difficult to observe in the model? ... in nature?

Assessment Goals

- Follow directions for setting up the model.
- Observe and identify water cycle processes in the model.
- Illustrate and label the parts of the natural water cycle.
- Write one or more paragraphs explaining the water cycle. Include the weather conditions the cycle causes.

Assessment Rubric

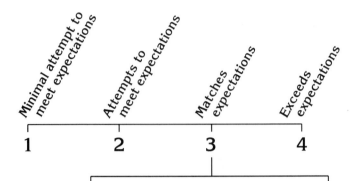

Minimal attempt to meet expectations	Attempts to meet expectations	Matches expectations	Exceeds expectations
1	2	3	4

Model
Follows directions for setting up model, uses materials appropriately

Observation
Uses correct language to identify processes observed, writing includes at least two observations

Illustration
Draws and labels a clearly recognizable scene showing evaporation, condensation, and precipitation

Explanation
Writes at least one paragraph explaining the water cycle; cites one weather condition for each part of the cycle (humidity, clouds, rain, etc.)

How does water move from Earth to sky and back?

Part One

Choose one of the following models.

Outdoors...
Materials

9 oz. wide-mouthed transparent cup
Black construction paper or brown paper towels
20 mL of water at room temperature
Ice cubes
Hand lens, optional

Place the paper on a concrete or asphalt surface. Pour the water into the center of the paper and cover with a transparent cup. Put an ice cube on top.

Indoors...
Materials

9 oz. wide-mouthed transparent cup
Plastic wrap
Hot water
Ice cubes
Hand lens, optional

Fill a transparent cup about 2 cm deep with hot water. Cover with plastic wrap, but not stretched tight. Place an ice cube on the plastic wrap.

Predict what will happen to the liquid water.

Record your observations using the language of science.

Part Two

On chart paper, draw and label a picture of the water cycle in nature. Also include at least one paragraph describing the water cycle and the weather conditions related to each part.

This culminating assessment is intended to follow the completion of activities in the two volumes of *Weather Sense*. It is keyed to the measurement learning goal presented in the front of both books:
- Construct and/or use meteorological tools, such as thermometers, psychrometers, anemometers, and barometers, to quantify observations.

Topic
Weather tools assessment

Focus
Students will demonstrate their knowledge of the tools used in *Weather Sense* in a matching format with problem-solving features.

Assessment Goals
- Match each *Weather Sense* tool with the attribute it measures and the measurement units that are customarily used.
- Match each Celsius thermometer with the appropriate weather story.
- Read 1- and 2-degree scales.
- Use a table.
- Know Celsius benchmarks for hot, cold, and comfortable temperatures.
- Write a weather story for one of the Celsius thermometers.

Guiding Documents
Project 2061 Benchmark
- *When people care about what is being counted or measured, it is important for them to say what the units are (three degrees Fahrenheit is different from three centimeters, three miles from three miles per hour).*

NRC Standards
- *Weather changes from day to day and over the seasons. Weather can be described by measurable quantities, such as temperature, wind direction and speed, and precipitation.*
- *Technology used to gather data enhances accuracy and allows scientists to analyze and quantify results of investigations.*

NCTM Standards 2000*
- *Understand the need for measuring with standard units and become familiar with standard units in the customary and metric systems*
- *Select and apply appropriate standard units and tools to measure length, area, volume, weight, time, temperature, and the size of angles*
- *Select and use benchmarks to estimate measurements*

Math
Measurement
    reading scales
    temperature benchmarks
Problem solving

Science
Earth science
    meteorology

Technology
Tools

Integrated Processes
Observing
Interpreting data
Relating

Materials
Scissors
Glue

Background Information
Measuring tools are a key means of gathering weather data. Students must be able to identify scale increments in order to accurately read the measurements. As the elements of weather are investigated, experience is gained measuring temperature with a thermometer, then air pressure with a barometer, and later wind direction with a wind vane, wind speed with a protractor anemometer, relative humidity with a sling psychrometer, and precipitation with a rain gauge. Through repeated measurements, a person acquires a growing sense of benchmarks for the various metric and customary scales—what is normal, what is low, what is high.

Since temperature is often the primary information wanted from a weather forecast, the thermometer's scale was chosen for the problem-solving portion of this assessment.

One other note: wind direction refers to a position in space, rather than a point on a numeric scale. Informally, however, the compass rose can be thought of as a scale and the north-south-east-west directions as a special kind of measurement unit.

Procedure

1. Remind students that over several weeks or months they have been measuring the weather with tools, some homemade and some commercial. Now you want to know what they have learned from using these tools.

2. Distribute the page with the concentric circles. From the listed choices, ask students to write the attribute and measurement units that are related to each tool.

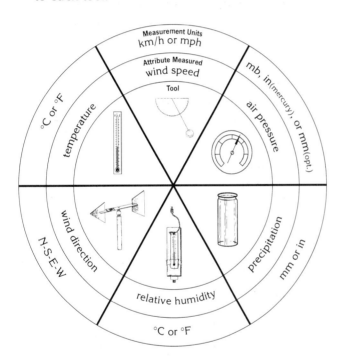

Optionally, have students name the weather tools. [Starting clockwise at the top: protractor anemometer, barometer, rain gauge, sling psychrometer, wind vane, thermometer]

3. Give each student the next two pages. Explain that they will read the weather story and cut and glue the appropriate thermometer(s) next to the story. *Answers:*
   1. It is a pleasant day with few clouds, warm enough to comfortably wear a T-shirt. [22°C]
   2. Whew, I'm sweaty! Let's go swimming and have some ice cream later. [39°C]
   3. The sun is out and, even though it is not very warm, the towels on the clothesline are drying. That's because the relative humidity is only 36%. What are the dry-bulb and wet-bulb temperatures? [dry-bulb: 15°C and wet-bulb: 8°C (Notice the table requires finding the difference between the two, 7°.]

4. Have students write an original weather story to match one or both of the remaining thermometers. [The remaining thermometers register 1°C and 11°C.]

5. Guide the sharing of stories.

Discussion

1. What story clues helped you find the matching thermometer? [1—pleasant, few clouds, warm enough to wear shorts; 2—sweaty, swimming, ice cream; 3—sun out, not very warm, towels drying, 36% relative humidity]

2. What else, besides temperature clues, did you need to know to pick the right thermometer? [which scale was used, what is hot and cold in Celsius]

3. How did you think through choosing the dry-bulb and wet-bulb temperatures for the third story?

Evidence of Learning

1. Observe the appropriate matching of the tool with the attribute measured and the metric and customary measuring units used.

2. Watch for appropriate matching of thermometer(s) to weather story.

3. Listen for reasonable explanations of the thinking process involved in choosing the right thermometer. Using story three as an example, did students reason that the thermometers must be between 0 and 16 because "not very warm" would be below 20°C and because the table is limited to those numbers?

* Reprinted with permission from *Principles and Standards for School Mathematics,* 2000 by the National Council of Teachers of Mathematics. All rights reserved.

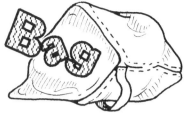

Weather Tool Bag

Write the attribute and measurement units matching each tool in the wheel.

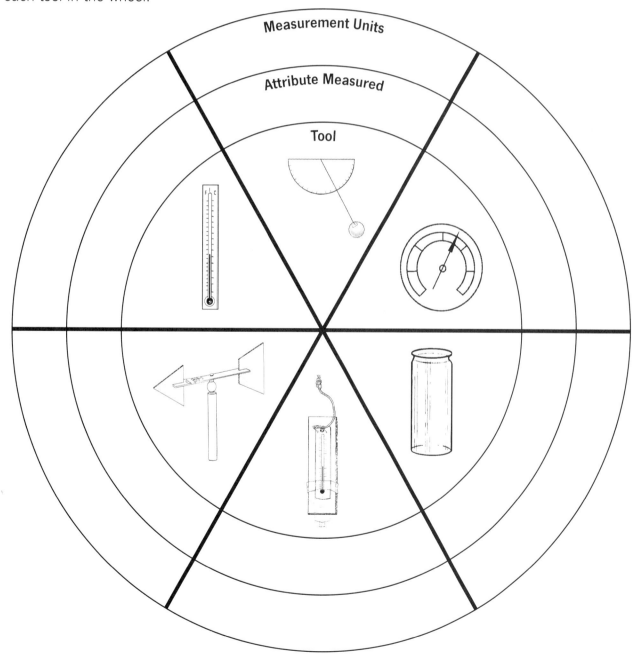

Measurement Units

Attribute Measured

Tool

Weather Tool Bag

1. It is a pleasant day with few clouds, warm enough to comfortably wear a T-shirt.

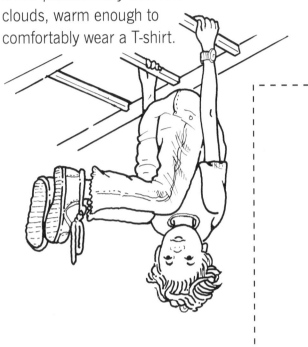

2. Whew, I'm sweaty! Let's go swimming and have some ice cream later.

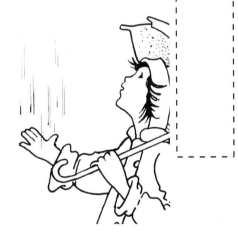

3. The sun is out and, even though it is not very warm, the towels on the clothesline are drying. That's because the relative humidity is only 36%. What are the dry-bulb and wet-bulb temperatures?

4. Write your own weather story to match one or both of the remaining thermometers.

Weather Tool Bag

Cut and glue the appropriate thermometer(s)
with the matching weather story.

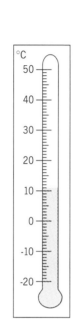
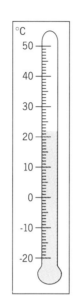
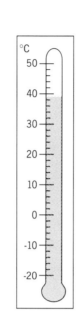
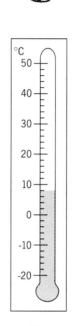
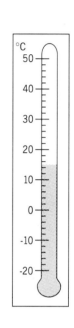

Relative Humidity Table

Difference between wet- and dry-bulb temperatures (C°)

Dry-Bulb Temperature (C°)	1	2	3	4	5	6	7	8	9	10
0	81	64	46	29	13					
1	83	66	49	33	17					
2	84	68	52	37	22	7				
3	84	70	55	40	26	12				
4	85	71	57	43	29	16				
5	86	72	58	45	33	20	7			
6	86	73	60	48	35	24	11			
7	87	74	62	50	38	26	15			
8	87	75	63	51	40	29	19	8		
9	88	76	64	53	42	32	22	12		
10	88	77	66	55	44	34	24	15	6	
11	89	78	67	56	46	36	27	18	9	
12	89	78	68	58	48	39	29	21	12	
13	89	79	69	59	50	41	32	23	15	7
14	90	79	70	60	51	42	34	26	18	10
15	90	80	71	61	53	44	36	27	20	13
16	90	81	71	63	54	46	38	30	23	15

Weather Literature

General Fisher, Aileen. *Always Wondering*. HarperCollins. New York. 1991. (The last section of this book, "Whoever Planned the World," has several wonderful poems having to do with weather.)

Kahl, Jonathan D. W. *National Audubon Society First Field Guide: Weather*. Scholastic, Inc. New York. 1998. (An introduction to weather, loaded with photographs and information. Includes a pictorial field guide card for handy identification of phenomena.)

Yolen, Jane, ed. *Weather Report: Poems Selected by Jane Yolen*. Boyds Mills Press (A Highlights Co.). Honesdale, PA. 1993. (Inviting poetry organized around the topics of rain, sun, wind, snow, and fog.)

Temperature Silverstein, Shel. "Here Comes," "Come Skating," "Tryin' on Clothes," and "It's Hot!" from *A Light in the Attic*. Harper & Row. New York. 1981. (Poetry with a unique twist of humor.)

Wind Bauer, Caroline Feller, ed. *Windy Day, Stories and Poems*. J.B. Lippincott. New York. 1988. (Delightful titles such as "While You Were Chasing a Hat!" and "The Bagel" are found in this collection of stories and poems.)

Calhoun, Mary. *Jack and the Whoopee Wind*. William Morrow. New York. 1987. (A whimsical tall tale about Cowboy Jack's attempts to stop the wind from blowing everything away. Great fun.)

Carlstrom, Nancy White. *How Does the Wind Walk?* Macmillan. New York. 1993. (Simple but poetic words and colorful illustrations about a young boy encountering the effects of the wind in each of the seasons.)

Ets, Marie Hall. *Gilberto and the Wind*. Viking Press. New York. 1963. (A young boy experiences the playfulness of wind in different settings and at different times of the year.)

Kennedy, Dorothy M., ed. *Make Things Fly: Poems about the Wind*. Margaret K. McElderry Books (Simon & Schuster). 1998. (This collection of poems includes two appealing activity-openers, "Crick! Crack!" by Eve Merriam and "The Wind" by John Ciardi.)

MacDonald, Elizabeth. *The Very Windy Day*. Tambourine Books (William Morrow). New York. 1991. (An amusing story in which the wind blows a hat and other objects away from people, passing the objects from person to person, and eventually returning them to their owners.)

McKissack, Patricia C. *Mirandy and Brother Wind*. Alfred A. Knopf. New York. 1988. (Mirandy tries to capture Brother Wind so that he can be her partner in the Junior Cakewalk Dance Contest.)

Silverstein, Shel. "Strange Wind" from *A Light in the Attic*. Harper & Row. New York. 1981. (Poetry with a unique twist of humor.)

Water Cycle   Branley, Franklin M. *Down Comes the Rain*. Scholastic, Inc. New York. 2000. (Drawn pictures explain evaporation, condensation, and precipitation. Though the look is primary, conceptually it is appropriate for middle grades too.)

Markert, Jenny. *Water*. Creative Education, Inc. Mankato, MN. 1992. (Informative text and gorgeous full-page colored photographs of scenes illustrating the water cycle as well as weathering caused by water in both its solid and liquid forms.)

McKinney, Barbara Shaw. *A Drop Around the World*. Dawn Publications. Nevada City, CA. 1998. (Colorful drawings and narrative in the form of verse illustrate how a drop of water is recycled over and over again—forming clouds, falling as rain, carried in the ocean, freezing into snowflakes, melting, soaking into soil, taken in by trees, floating in the jet stream, becoming vapor in a rain forest, etc.—as it travels around the world. A natural connection to geography from Australia to Japan, from the Sahara to the Arctic. Excellent for middle grades.)

Walker, Sally M. *Water Up, Water Down: The Hydrologic Cycle*. Carolrhoda Books, Inc. Minneapolis. 1992. (Beautiful photographs accompany a text explaining the water cycle.)

Wick, Walter. *A Drop of Water*. Scholastic Press. Jefferson City, MO. 1996.
(Text and wonderful photographs that illustrate the properties of water as well as the water cycle. Includes snowflakes, condensation, and evaporation. Suitable for middle grades and beyond.)

Clouds   Ariane. *Small Cloud*. Walker and Company. New York. 1996. (An endearing tale of the birth of a cloud, its travels, and how it eventually fed the Earth with rain, completing a journey through the water cycle.)

Harper, Suzanne. *Clouds: From Mare's Tails to Thunderheads*. Franklin Watts. New York. 1997. (Basic information about clouds with text and photographs given about equal space.)

Lustig, Michael and Esther. *Willy Whyner, Cloud Designer*. Four Winds Press (Macmillan). New York. 1994. (A fantasy about a third-grade boy who makes unusual kinds of clouds. Tongue-in-cheek humor.)

McMillan, Bruce. *The Weather Sky*. Farrar Straus Giroux. New York. 1991. (Various kinds of clouds are introduced, each featured on a page with a color photograph, paragraph of text, and an altitude graph showing its relative position in the sky. For upper elementary and above.)

Markert, Jenny. *Clouds*. Creative Education, Inc. Mankato, MN. 1992. (Brief but informative text and gorgeous full-page colored photographs of the three types of clouds and associated weather phenomena. An excellent introduction for elementary students.)

de Paola, Tomie. *The Cloud Book*. Holiday House. New York. 1985 (reissue). (Cloud descriptions and a few weather proverbs provide the text for the colorful illustrations.)

Silverstein, Shel. "Arrows" from *A Light in the Attic*. Harper & Row. New York. 1981. (Poetry with a unique twist of humor.)

Rain

Bauer, Caroline Feller, ed. *Rainy Day, Stories and Poems.* HarperCollins. New York. 1986. (A collection with titles such as "Rain-Walking," "Rain Sizes," and "Cloudy with a Chance of Meatballs.")

Buchanan, Ken & Debby. *It Rained on the Desert Today.* Northland Publishing. Flagstaff, AZ. 1994. (The anticipation and wonder of a desert rain seen through the eyes of children. Beautiful watercolor illustrations. A "Reading Rainbow" book.)

Cobb, Vicki. *This Place is Dry.* Walker and Co. New York. 1989. (Become immersed in the dry climate, plants, and animals of Arizona's Sonoran Desert.)

Cobb, Vicki. *This Place is Wet.* Walker and Co. New York. 1989. (Colored drawings and text help you experience life in the Brazilian Rain Forest—the humid, wet climate, the people, the plants, and the animals.)

Silverstein, Shel. "Snap!" from *A Light in the Attic.* Harper & Row. New York. 1981. (Poetry with a unique twist of humor.)

Silverstein, Shel. "Rain" and "Lazy Jane" from *Where the Sidewalk Ends.* Harper & Row. New York. 1974. (Humorous poetry.)

Spier, Peter. *Rain.* Zephyr. Somerville, MA. 1987. (Two children enjoy the rain in this wordless book.)

Snow

Bauer, Caroline Feller, editor. *Snowy Day, Stories and Poems.* HarperCollins. New York. 1986. (A collection of short stories, poems, and a recipe or two to capture the imagination.)

Bianchi, John and Frank B. Edwards. *Snow.* Bungalo Books. Newburgh, Ontario, Canada or Firefly Books Inc. Buffalo, NY. 1992. (Inviting illustrations and varied content, from snowshoes to igloos to animals, draw you into "learning for the fun of it," the book's subtitle.)

Martin, Jacqueline Briggs. *Snowflake Bentley.* Houghton Mifflin. Boston. 1998. (Winner of the 1998 Caldecott Medal, this book introduces children to Wilson Bentley whose hobby was photographing snowflakes, thousands of them, in the early 1900s. Illustrated by Mary Azarian.)

McSwigan, Marie. *Snow Treasure.* Scholastic, Inc. New York. 1997 (reissue). (A suspenseful, though probably fictional, story set in Norway during World War II. Using the snowy winter landscape and their sleds, Norwegian children slip thousands of dollars of gold bricks past the German invaders.)

Prelutsky, Jack. *It's Snowing! It's Snowing!* Greenwillow Books. New York. 1984. (Whimsical poetry about everyday happenings in cold weather. Includes titles such as "The Snowman's Lament," "Stuck in the Snow," and "My Mother Took Me Skating." Perfect for middle grades.)

Silverstein, Shel. "Snowman" from *Where the Sidewalk Ends.* Harper & Row. New York. 1974. (Humorous poetry.)

Look for *The Winter of the Blue Snow,* a very short story about spoken words freezing in mid-air, in a number of books about Paul Bunyan.

Reference Books for Teachers

Ludlum, David M. *The Audubon Society Field Guide to North American Weather.* Alfred A. Knopf. New York. 1991. (Concise explanations, photographs to aid identification of clouds and other weather phenomena, information on weather instruments and the station model, etc.)

Williams, Jack. *The Weather Book (USA Today®).* Vintage Books (Random House, Inc.). New York. 1992. (Explanations and extensive graphics make the complexities of weather understandable. If you only get one reference, this is the one to have.)

Weather Websites

For National Weather Service station sites:
        NOAA   http://www.nws.noaa.gov/organization.html

        NOAA   http://www.wrh.noaa.gov/wrhq/nwspage.html

For background information on weather:
        USA Today   http://www.usatoday.com/weather/

For current weather conditions:
        Accu-Weather   http://www.accuweather.com

        BBC Weather Centre   http://www.bbc.co.uk/weather/

        Intellicast   http://www.intellicast.com

        USA Today   http://www.usatoday.com/weather/

        The Weather Channel   http://www.weather.com

        WeatherNet   http://cirrus.sprl.umich.edu/wxnet/

        Weather Underground   http://www.wunderground.com

For snow data:
        Snow-forecast.com   http://www.snow-forecast.com

For monthly climate data:
        World Climate   http://www.WorldClimate.com

For weather calculators:
        NOAA   http://tgsv5.nws.noaa.gov/er/box/calculate2.html

Correct at time of publication.

The AIMS Program

AIMS is the acronym for "**A**ctivities **I**ntegrating **M**athematics and **S**cience." Such integration enriches learning and makes it meaningful and holistic. AIMS began as a project of Fresno Pacific University to integrate the study of mathematics and science in grades K-9, but has since expanded to include language arts, social studies, and other disciplines.

AIMS is a continuing program of the non-profit AIMS Education Foundation. It had its inception in a National Science Foundation funded program whose purpose was to explore the effectiveness of integrating mathematics and science. The project directors in cooperation with 80 elementary classroom teachers devoted two years to a thorough field-testing of the results and implications of integration.

The approach met with such positive results that the decision was made to launch a program to create instructional materials incorporating this concept. Despite the fact that thoughtful educators have long recommended an integrative approach, very little appropriate material was available in 1981 when the project began. A series of writing projects have ensued and today the AIMS Education Foundation is committed to continue the creation of new integrated activities on a permanent basis.

The AIMS program is funded through the sale of this developing series of books and proceeds from the Foundation's endowment. All net income from program and products flows into a trust fund administered by the AIMS Education Foundation. Use of these funds is restricted to support of research, development, and publication of new materials. Writers donate all their rights to the Foundation to support its on-going program. No royalties are paid to the writers.

The rationale for integration lies in the fact that science, mathematics, language arts, social studies, etc., are integrally interwoven in the real world from which it follows that they should be similarly treated in the classroom where we are preparing students to live in that world. Teachers who use the AIMS program give enthusiastic endorsement to the effectiveness of this approach.

Science encompasses the art of questioning, investigating, hypothesizing, discovering, and communicating. Mathematics is a language that provides clarity, objectivity, and understanding. The language arts provide us powerful tools of communication. Many of the major contemporary societal issues stem from advancements in science and must be studied in the context of the social sciences. Therefore, it is timely that all of us take seriously a more holistic mode of educating our students. This goal motivates all who are associated with the AIMS Program. We invite you to join us in this effort.

Meaningful integration of knowledge is a major recommendation coming from the nation's professional science and mathematics associations. The American Association for the Advancement of Science in *Science for All Americans* strongly recommends the integration of mathematics, science, and technology. The National Council of Teachers of Mathematics places strong emphasis on applications of mathematics such as are found in science investigations. AIMS is fully aligned with these recommendations.

Extensive field testing of AIMS investigations confirms these beneficial results.

1. Mathematics becomes more meaningful, hence more useful, when it is applied to situations that interest students.
2. The extent to which science is studied and understood is increased, with a significant economy of time, when mathematics and science are integrated.
3. There is improved quality of learning and retention, supporting the thesis that learning which is meaningful and relevant is more effective.
4. Motivation and involvement are increased dramatically as students investigate real-world situations and participate actively in the process.

We invite you to become part of this classroom teacher movement by using an integrated approach to learning and sharing any suggestions you may have. The AIMS Program welcomes you!

AIMS Education Foundation Programs

A Day with AIMS®

Intensive one-day workshops are offered to introduce educators to the philosophy and rationale of AIMS. Participants will discuss the methodology of AIMS and the strategies by which AIMS principles may be incorporated into curriculum. Each participant will take part in a variety of hands-on AIMS investigations to gain an understanding of such aspects as the scientific/mathematical content, classroom management, and connections with other curricular areas. *A Day with AIMS®* workshops may be offered anywhere in the United States. Necessary supplies and take-home materials are usually included in the enrollment fee.

A Week with AIMS®

Throughout the nation, AIMS offers many one-week workshops each year, usually in the summer. Each workshop lasts five days and includes at least 30 hours of AIMS hands-on instruction. Participants are grouped according to the grade level(s) in which they are interested. Instructors are members of the AIMS Instructional Leadership Network. Supplies for the activities and a generous supply of take-home materials are included in the enrollment fee. Sites are selected on the basis of applications submitted by educational organizations. If chosen to host a workshop, the host agency agrees to provide specified facilities and cooperate in the promotion of the workshop. The AIMS Education Foundation supplies workshop materials as well as the travel, housing, and meals for instructors.

AIMS One-Week Perspectives Workshops

Each summer, Fresno Pacific University offers AIMS one-week workshops on its campus in Fresno, California. AIMS Program Directors and highly qualified members of the AIMS National Leadership Network serve as instructors.

The AIMS Instructional Leadership Program

This is an AIMS staff-development program seeking to prepare facilitators for leadership roles in science/math education in their home districts or regions. Upon successful completion of the program, trained facilitators may become members of the AIMS Instructional Leadership Network, qualified to conduct AIMS workshops, teach AIMS in-service courses for college credit, and serve as AIMS consultants. Intensive training is provided in mathematics, science, process and thinking skills, workshop management, and other relevant topics.

College Credit and Grants

Those who participate in workshops may often qualify for college credit. If the workshop takes place on the campus of Fresno Pacific University, that institution may grant appropriate credit. If the workshop takes place off-campus, arrangements can sometimes be made for credit to be granted by another institution. In addition, the applicant's home school district is often willing to grant in-service or professional-development credit. Many educators who participate in AIMS workshops are recipients of various types of educational grants, either local or national. Nationally known foundations and funding agencies have long recognized the value of AIMS mathematics and science workshops to educators. The AIMS Education Foundation encourages educators interested in attending or hosting workshops to explore the possibilities suggested above. Although the Foundation strongly supports such interest, it reminds applicants that they have the primary responsibility for fulfilling *current* requirements.

For current information regarding the programs described above, please complete the following:

Information Request

Please send current information on the items checked:

____ *Basic Information Packet* on AIMS materials ____*A Week with AIMS®* workshops
____ *AIMS Instructional Leadership Program*   ____Hosting information for *A Day with AIMS®* workshops
____ *AIMS One-Week Perspectives* workshops   ____Hosting information for *A Week with AIMS®* workshops

Name _____ Phone _____

Address _____
       Street   City   State   Zip

We invite you to subscribe to *AIMS*®!

Each issue of *AIMS*® contains a variety of material useful to educators at all grade levels. Feature articles of lasting value deal with topics such as mathematical or science concepts, curriculum, assessment, the teaching of process skills, and historical background. Several of the latest AIMS math/science investigations are always included, along with their reproducible activity sheets. As needs direct and space allows, various issues contain news of current developments, such as workshop schedules, activities of the AIMS Instructional Leadership Network, and announcements of upcoming publications.

AIMS® is published monthly, August through May. Subscriptions are on an annual basis only. A subscription entered at any time will begin with the next issue, but will also include the previous issues of that volume. Readers have preferred this arrangement because articles and activities within an annual volume are often interrelated.

Please note that an *AIMS*® subscription automatically includes duplication rights for one school site for all issues included in the subscription. Many schools build cost-effective library resources with their subscriptions.

YES! I am interested in subscribing to *AIMS*®.

Name _____ Home Phone _____

Address _____ City, State, Zip _____

Please send the following volumes (subject to availability):

_____ Volume VIII	(1993-94)	$15.00		_____ Volume XIII	(1998-99)	$30.00
_____ Volume IX	(1994-95)	$15.00		_____ Volume XIV	(1999-00)	$30.00
_____ Volume X	(1995-96)	$15.00		_____ Volume XV	(2000-01)	$30.00
_____ Volume XI	(1996-97)	$30.00		_____ Volume XVI	(2001-02)	$30.00
_____ Volume XII	(1997-98)	$30.00		_____ Volume XVII	(2002-03)	$30.00

_____ **Limited offer: Volumes XVII & XVIII (2002-2004) $55.00**
(Note: Prices may change without notice)

Check your method of payment:

☐ Check enclosed in the amount of $_____

☐ Purchase order attached (Please include the P.O.#, the authorizing signature, and position of the authorizing person.)

☐ Credit Card   ☐ Visa   ☐ MasterCard   Amount $ _____

Card # _____   Expiration Date _____

Signature_____   Today's Date _____

Make checks payable to **AIMS Education Foundation.**
Mail to *AIMS*® Magazine, P.O. Box 8120, Fresno, CA 93747-8120.
Phone (559) 255-4094 or (888) 733-2467 FAX (559) 255-6396
AIMS Homepage: http://www.AIMSedu.org/

AIMS Program Publications

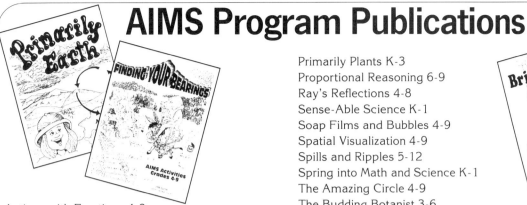

Actions with Fractions 4-9
Awesome Addition and Super Subtraction 2-3
Bats Incredible! 2-4
Brick Layers 4-9
Brick Layers II 4-9
Counting on Coins 1-2
Crazy about Cotton Book 3-7
Critters K-6
Cycles of Knowing and Growing 1-3
Down to Earth 5-9
Electrical Connections 4-9
Exploring Environments Book K-6
Fabulous Fractions 3-6
Fall into Math and Science K-1
Field Detectives 3-6
Finding Your Bearings 4-9
Floaters and Sinkers 5-9
From Head to Toe 5-9
Fun with Foods 5-9
Glide into Winter with Math & Science K-1
Gravity Rules! Activity Book 5-12
Hardhatting in a Geo-World 3-5
It's About Time K-2
Jaw Breakers and Heart Thumpers 3-5
Just for the Fun of It! 4-9
Looking at Lines 6-9
Machine Shop 5-9
Magnificent Microworld Adventures 5-9
Marvelous Multiplication and Dazzling Division 4-5
Math + Science, A Solution 5-9
Mostly Magnets 2-8
Multiplication the Algebra Way 4-8
Off The Wall Science 3-9
Our Wonderful World 5-9
Out of This World 4-8
Overhead and Underfoot 3-5
Paper Square Geometry: The Mathematics of Origami
Puzzle Play: 4-8
Pieces and Patterns 5-9
Popping With Power 3-5
Primarily Bears K-6
Primarily Earth K-3
Primarily Physics K-3

Primarily Plants K-3
Proportional Reasoning 6-9
Ray's Reflections 4-8
Sense-Able Science K-1
Soap Films and Bubbles 4-9
Spatial Visualization 4-9
Spills and Ripples 5-12
Spring into Math and Science K-1
The Amazing Circle 4-9
The Budding Botanist 3-6
The Sky's the Limit 5-9
Through the Eyes of the Explorers 5-9
Under Construction K-2
Water Precious Water 2-6
Weather Sense: Moisture 4-5
Weather Sense: Temperature, Air Pressure, and Wind 4-5
Winter Wonders K-2

Spanish/English Editions
Brinca de alegria hacia la Primavera con las
    Matemáticas y Ciencias K-1
Cáete de gusto hacia el Otoño con las
    Matemáticas y Ciencias K-1
Conexiones Eléctricas 4-9
El Botanista Principiante 3-6
Los Cinco Sentidos K-1
Ositos Nada Más K-6
Patine al Invierno con Matemáticas y Ciencias K-1
Piezas y Diseños 5-9
Primariamente Física K-3
Primariamente Plantas K-3
Principalmente Imanes 2-8

All Spanish/English Editions include student pages in
Spanish and teacher and student pages in English.

Spanish Edition
Constructores II: Ingeniería Creativa Con Construcciones LEGO® (4-9)
The entire book is written in Spanish. English pages not included.

Other Science and Math Publications
Historical Connections in Mathematics, Vol. I 5-9
Historical Connections in Mathematics, Vol. II 5-9
Historical Connections in Mathematics, Vol. III 5-9
Mathematicians are People, Too
Mathematicians are People, Too, Vol. II
Teaching Science with Everyday Things
What's Next, Volume 1, 4-12
What's Next, Volume 2, 4-12
What's Next, Volume 3, 4-12

For further information write to:
AIMS Education Foundation • P.O. Box 8120 • Fresno, California 93747-8120
www.AIMSedu.org/ • Fax 559•255•6396

AIMS Duplication Rights Program

AIMS has received many requests from school districts for the purchase of unlimited duplication rights to AIMS materials. In response, the AIMS Education Foundation has formulated the program outlined below. There is a built-in flexibility which, we trust, will provide for those who use AIMS materials extensively to purchase such rights for either individual activities or entire books.

It is the goal of the AIMS Education Foundation to make its materials and programs available at reasonable cost. All income from the sale of publications and duplication rights is used to support AIMS programs; hence, strict adherence to regulations governing duplication is essential. Duplication of AIMS materials beyond limits set by copyright laws and those specified below is strictly forbidden.

Limited Duplication Rights

Any purchaser of an AIMS book may make up to *200 copies* of any activity in that book for use at *one school site*. Beyond that, rights must be purchased according to the appropriate category.

Unlimited Duplication Rights for Single Activities

An individual or school may purchase the right to make an unlimited number of copies of a single activity. The royalty is $5.00 per activity per school site.

Examples: 3 activities x 1 site x $5.00 = $15.00
          9 activities x 3 sites x $5.00 = $135.00

Unlimited Duplication Rights for Entire Books

A school or district may purchase the right to make an unlimited number of copies of a single, *specified* book. The royalty is $20.00 per book per school site. This is in addition to the cost of the book.

Examples: 5 books x 1 site x $20.00 = $100.00
          12 books x 10 sites x $20.00 = $2400.00

Magazine/Newsletter Duplication Rights

Those who purchase *AIMS*® (magazine)/*Newsletter* are hereby granted permission to make up to 200 copies of any portion of it, provided these copies will be used for educational purposes.

Workshop Instructors' Duplication Rights

Workshop instructors may distribute to registered workshop participants a maximum of 100 copies of any article and/or 100 copies of no more than eight activities, provided these six conditions are met:

1. Since all AIMS activities are based upon the *AIMS Model of Mathematics* and the *AIMS Model of Learning,* leaders must include in their presentations an explanation of these two models.
2. Workshop instructors must relate the AIMS activities presented to these basic explanations of the AIMS philosophy of education.
3. The copyright notice must appear on all materials distributed.
4. Instructors must provide information enabling participants to order books and magazines from the Foundation.
5. Instructors must inform participants of their limited duplication rights as outlined below.
6. Only student pages may be duplicated.

Written permission must be obtained for duplication beyond the limits listed above. Additional royalty payments may be required.

Workshop Participants' Rights

Those enrolled in workshops in which AIMS student activity sheets are distributed may duplicate a maximum of 35 copies or enough to use the lessons one time with one class, whichever is less. Beyond that, rights must be purchased according to the appropriate category.

Application for Duplication Rights

The purchasing agency or individual must clearly specify the following:
1. Name, address, and telephone number
2. Titles of the books for Unlimited Duplication Rights contracts
3. Titles of activities for Unlimited Duplication Rights contracts
4. Names and addresses of school sites for which duplication rights are being purchased.

NOTE: Books to be duplicated must be purchased separately and are not included in the contract for Unlimited Duplication Rights.

The requested duplication rights are automatically authorized when proper payment is received, although a *Certificate of Duplication Rights* will be issued when the application is processed.

Address all correspondence to: **Contract Division**
AIMS Education Foundation   www.AIMSedu.org/
P.O. Box 8120   Fax 559•255•6396
Fresno, CA 93747-8120